HOW TO GET A GREAT JOB – AND KEEP IT!

Other titles by the same author:

Home Based Businesses for the Over-50's
ISBN Number: 0-646-45213-4
Publisher: J.V.M.Enterprises, Australlia

Poems in *Coastlines: Poems from Bayside* (2010)
ISBN 978-0-646-52831-1
Publisher: Coastlines, Australia

Judi Menzies'

HOW TO GET A
GREAT JOB
– AND *KEEP* IT!

2nd Edition

Includes Top Economist's forecast for
JOBS OF THE FUTURE!

J.V.M. Enterprises, P.O. Box 95, Brighton, Victoria 3186, Australia

Typeset by BookPOD

DISCLAIMER:

The author cannot and does not guarantee nor provide any warranty that any of the ideas or suggestions offered in this book, written predominately for *the Australian jobseekers' market*, will produce any particular outcome for any particular person as everybody's circumstances and abilities will differ. Neither the author nor the contributors assume any liability of any kind with respect to the accuracy or completeness of the contents of this publication.

Before commencing any career action it is not only prudent but essential to understand the legal, regulatory and management issues relevant to your particular circumstances by seeking and obtaining appropriate professional advice.

ISBN: 978-0-646-34913-8

A catalogue record for this book is available from the National Library of Australia

NATIONAL LIBRARY OF AUSTRALIA

ACKNOWLEDGEMENTS

The author is indebted to
Dr. Stan Rodski (psychologist),
Phil Ruthven (economic forecaster)
and to the network of recruiters who
offered their selfless input.

Contents

PART THREE: HOW TO KEEP THAT GREAT JOB

PART FOUR: SELF-EMPLOYMENT WOULD IT WORK FOR YOU?

PART FIVE: JOBS OF THE FUTURE

PART SIX: DO-IT-YOURSELF RESUME GUIDE

INTRODUCTION

*'... if you bake bread with indifference, you bake a
bitter bread that feeds but half man's hunger.'*

- KAHLIL GIBRAN, *THE PROPHET*

The aim of this book is to prove to you that you don't have to settle for a second rate job or no job at all when a 'great' job is only a few steps away.

The majority of people spend their working days unsatisfied, unchallenged or just plain miserable for the benefit of receiving a weekly pay cheque. They get up at dawn, trudge off to the office, factory or shop, then come home when day is over wondering what life is all about.

Thousands don't even have a job and despair of ever getting one. Is it any wonder that there is so much stress and tension in society? Yet finding a job that is both satisfying and fulfilling is not at all difficult...*if* you go about it the right way.

Merely responding to a few ads and sending out resumes won't get you a job unless you're very lucky! It certainly won't get you a *great* job. *Great* jobs need to be targeted as neatly and as narrowly as you would aim an arrow at a bull's-eye!

In fact, job hunting is a bit like a contest: there are the contestants... and then there is the 'prize': the prize is the job.

1

Given a neck-on-neck race with an equally talented opponent, anyone who has learned the rules of the competition and adopted the most appropriate strategies will end up the winner hands-down.

This manual gives you the rules of the game and the winning strategies you'll need. As well, it touches on a few 'peripheral' subjects considered complementary to both job search and job maintenance such as coping with retrenchment, ways of *keeping* your 'great job' when you find it, the main avenues of *self-employment*...and even a peek into the workplace of the future revealed by one of Australia's most highly respected economic forecasters.

Be confident about following the information presented to you in these pages. It has been drawn from recruitment consultants, psychologists, economists and other professionals who have had years of experience in the recruitment industry and commerce.

It can work miracles for you - if you will give it a chance.

PART ONE

IF YOU'VE LOST
YOUR JOB...

HOW TO COPE WITH JOB LOSS – AND WIN!

Many people lose their jobs these days through no fault of their own. Increasingly clever technology is creeping in to replace human effort in almost every field!

When loss of a job is due to computerisation or the adoption of new systems, it is particularly difficult to cope with. It means that no matter how good your job performance has been, if the work itself has become redundant there will be no similar job offering as a replacement - unless you change careers. For younger, more adaptable workers this is a possibility but for those who have put their lives and experience into one particular area, it can be devastating.

Consulting psychologist and career counselor, Dr. Stan Rodski of Melbourne, is regarded as a 'survival tactitian' in the field of retrenchment counseling. He says today's *official* unemployment rate does not reflect real numbers because thousands of retrenchees refuse to register, going to extraordinary lengths to hide the fact they are jobless.

"Being faced with the loss of your livelihood and the wherewithal to support your family is similar to being told a loved one has been killed in an accident", he says. "The first reaction is sheer disbelief".

Retrenchees generally go through a definite four-stage 'grieving cycle', he explains: first denial, then anger followed by depression and finally, hope.

The denial phase can even involve keeping the news from the family. Stories of the retrenched executive who pretends to go off to work each morning...only to spend the day on a park bench or walking aimlessly around shopping centres are only too common, says Rodski. "You need to be direct with family and friends - and get it over and done with," he says.

Undoubtedly, confronting the problem like this will give rise to anger. Retrenchees start asking questions like: "Why has the organisation got itself to this point?" or "Why didn't they warn me eight months ago about this when I could have worked out some procedure to improve my options?"

"You get angry at everyone at this point," says Rodski. "How long it goes on depends on the individual and the circumstances. Of course, where preventative measures could have been taken by the firm, and weren't, anger is an appropriate reaction," he says.

Soon, however, one realises the uselessness of projecting anger outward: "we can write all the letters we like to the MD and call him all the things we want...but it's not going to change a thing!"

It is at this stage that the retrenchee moves into the third and most vicious part of the cycle, says Rodski: *depression*. "Here, the anger becomes internalized and one's energy is forced into such negative thoughts as 'this is my fault! I brought it on myself!'

Retrenchees can become moody and withdrawn at this point...and extremely dangerous to themselves."

What happens from then on will depend on a number of factors such as the closeness of the family, the strength of your network of friends...and, to a large extent, on your own psychological make-up and personal resolve. Financial stability and the size of your retrenchment package will also be key factors.

We hear of huge severance packages being handed out at the top level of the market place, suggesting that senior executives fare better than their more junior counterparts in retrenchment. But age and lack of flexibility often make it harder for senior men or women to find another position. 'Last-on/first-off' retrenchees may receive only a small severance pay and short notice but, on the other hand, it could be said they don't have to contend with quite the same emotional bonds.

The extent to which employers will go in providing outplacement support varies widely. While tt is acknowledged as being invaluable in giving retrenchees a set procedure to follow at a time of great confusion and emotional turmoil, it gives no guarantee of finding them replacement jobs. Where outplacement assistance is not offered, there are many relevant self-help groups that are freely available...which provide peer support and much-needed motivation in accessing resources.

"The individual who avails himself of a self-help group or outplacement assistance will have a distinct advantage over someone trying to go it alone", says Rodski, "because suddenly, there's a network - usually with a professional worker showing interest and guiding you back on track.

"Job-seekers who have been out of work for months - even a year or more - lining up, sending out resumes, waiting, hoping...then failing once more to land a job can plunge back to the beginning of the four-stage cycle of denial, anger, depression and renewed hope. There's a point where some just give up. They may end up on the phone to Lifeline or move to drugs or alcohol!"

Or...they can follow the advice in this book! In the following pages, we show you ways of getting a great job - and *keeping* it. But we urge you to be realistic in acknowledging the many changes occurring in today's job market. You may find you, too, have to change in order to adapt. This will not be easy for those who have spent their lives gaining expertise in fields that are now disappearing into technology's trash can. But hopefully you will come to see the truth of the well-known saying: "When one door closes, another one opens."

By the time you reach the final chapter, *Jobs of the Future*, you will see that nobody with a bit of spunk and 'get-up-and-go' need fear this new millennium.

PART TWO

HOW TO GET A *GREAT* JOB

WHAT *IS* A 'GREAT' JOB?

How do you define *a great job*? Do you measure its attractiveness in dollar terms, in hours of labour, in job satisfaction?

For a moment, visualize yourself as having attained the summit of business success. You possess power and influence, vast income, palatial homes, shares, gold and property. How does it feel?

See yourself sitting at a meeting of the Board, addressing the members. As you cast your eye over your itinerary and the expansive plans you are about to implement, think about the type of make-or-break financial decisions you will be expected to make.

Would you feel comfortable in an equivalent working environment with its non-stop, high pressure decision-making and level of responsibility? Do you believe you could cope intellectually, emotionally and physically with such a job?

For a few people, a position like that with its rewards of great wealth and power would be a dream. But it would plunge the average man or woman into confusion, stress and feelings of utter inadequacy. Unfortunately wealth comes at a price. The elite business exemplars who smile from the glossy pages of *Fortune 500* have generally paid dearly for their positions at the top. They live and breathe corporate life with its never-ending demands and long working hours. They have become imbued with an infallible determination to succeed under all circumstances, shrugging off the kicks and put-downs of competitors and showing a willingness to take risks that even Houdini might have avoided.

All of us want riches... but dollars alone aren't always sufficient reward for one's labour. Take a look in any investment or business opportunities magazine to test this statement. There you will inevitably find a plethora of ads offering to show you how 'you can become your own boss' earning sums like $36,000 in 30 days by working for 'just a few hours per day'! Another ad in a US business magazine offers to teach people 'how to make $5000 every time you take *one quick phone call*'!

Such ads throw up an interesting phenomenon that we sometimes tend to overlook: that even the possibility of making a figure like $36,000 per month is not sufficient inducement in itself to entice 'get-rich-quick' job seekers! People want *more* than money... and experienced advertisers understand very well what it is they *do* want: to successfully drag in recruits, the ads must offer superior (although often impossible-to-achieve) *lifestyle* benefits as well.

The following is the style of ad that sells franchises and business opportunities. Is it really so hard to see why?'

'I made myself a millionaire in a year lying under a palm tree on a tropical island. You can do it, too!'

Adequate remuneration is obviously necessary in order to keep oneself and one's family alive - but superior remuneration is not always sufficient inducement in itself to force one to change jobs.

Great jobs cannot always be measured in dollar terms. There are many other factors that could add to or subtract from their value to you. Furthermore, there is no uniformity of appeal when it comes to assessing those values. What one person sees as 'great' may be loathsome to another. A busy medical specialist hates his job and longs to work from home as a full-time artist: "What's money', he says, "if I never get time to be with my wife and children or do the things I really enjoy in life?" Yet his patients shake their heads and mutter enviously to each other, "Huh! How'd you like a job like that? $280 for just 20 minutes!"

If you are not satisfied with the job you have, you are in good company. The incredible statistics show that:

> **'as few as 4 out of 10 people truly enjoy**
> **what they're doing to earn a living!'**

> **P. RUTHVEN, IBISWORLD BUSINESS**
> **& INFORMATION SERVICES**

This means sixty percent of the workforce unwillingly drags itself off to work each day, secretly wishing for another life. Others passively accept job dissatisfaction as their 'fate' - be it through lack of education, lack of opportunity for advancement or adverse personal circumstances. Some fear to change jobs because they fear change itself. There are also those who lack confidence in themselves, are too lazy to move or are simply ill-informed on how to go about altering their present circumstances. However, as the saying goes:

'If you always do what you've always done...
You'll always get what you've always got!'

UNKNOWN

Higher achievement is often underrated or deferred until it is too late. Workers can become resigned to stagnation, thus condemning themselves to a lifetime functioning as a cog in a company wheel churning out profits for someone else as if they were trapped in a time warp in the Industrial Revolution.

This is not to suggest that all employees should immediately down tools and go into their own businesses. But it does suggest we should extract the best we can out of life by taking or making opportunities that satisfy us as human beings while we have the chance.

"I've never had a lucky break in my life" disgruntled workers may say -but this is no excuse because, believe it or not, Lady Luck loves to work for you! She only needs a little inducement, performing her magic the moment she sees planning, self-education, dedication, enthusiasm, opportunity-seeking and the willingness to take an occasional calculated risk. Then she delights in performing miracles for you.

Even if you love the type of work you do, you may not like what goes with it. For example, the management culture may be impossible to live with or your superiors may be corporate vampires who are constantly taking the credit for your creative genius! This is a common problem. What can you do about it? Continue to scream in silence...or dare you speak up?

While your present working life may appear unrewarding, spare a thought for the *unemployed*. Some have been out of work for years despite having had scores of job interviews. Unfortunately, society is not overly generous in its support for the out-of-work and their families, so these people suffer not only financially but in terms of decaying self-esteem and self-worth as well. Some parents watch their children grow up with only the bare necessities and wonder if there will ever be a chance to provide them with a better life.

As Dr. Stan Rodski pointed out in the previous chapter, the jobless in our society are far more numerous than is generally realized. Thousands of retrenchees prefer not to register for unemployment and often go to extraordinary lengths to hide the fact they are without a job.

Whether you are currently unemployed, in a job you dislike... or merely feel you would do better in another environment, this manual will show you that you *can* get a great job that's satisfying, stimulating and rewarding... *if* you know how to go about it.

The fuel of success is a potent mix of honest self-assessment, market research, strategic planning and action - and you need a constant supply of these things as you head toward your clearly defined goal. Don't doubt yourself for one minute! You *can* do it... and this book will show you *how*.

All jobseekers - no matter at what level - will benefit by reading this manual thoroughly and doing all the written exercises before presenting themselves on the job front. This will give you a new perspective on a) what you want, b) what you have to offer in terms of immediate, future and potential ability...and c) where you are likely to find the most rewarding and fulfilling environment for expressing your talent.

Basically, there are two ways to approach job search: passively and actively. If you take the passive approach, you will wait until you hear or read of a suitable position - maybe on computer job sites or social media, in newspaper or magazines or even through the 'grapevine'- before taking any action. (Don't hold your breath!)

On the other hand, if you take the *active* approach, you'll go out and purposefully MARKET yourself! By doing so, you will see that selling your talent is not difficult - once you know how to go about it.

Remember, in job hunting, you are your own merchandise: you need to be well displayed, in the right market... and offered by the vendor with the greatest vested interest in your success: YOU!

Members of some professions depend on constant self-marketing even to survive. The majority of well-known and highly paid screen actors or top models, for example, would be unknown today if they had shied away from self-marketing.

Generally, such people - no matter how famous or talented - have had to do the rounds of agencies, producers and promoters for many years. Even the greatest of them face fierce competition and rigorous auditioning for top roles. The audience sees only the final glamorous result - but the star knows how much it costs to twinkle on that big screen!

Bright, ambitious people who have confidence in their ability and who are always on the lookout for new career challenges generally say they enjoy the self-marketing that is so necessary for advancement. These people:

- define what they want
- assess the relevancy of their skills and knowledge
- research or 'engineer' job opportunities
- target the most likely 'buyer' of their services
- inform themselves fully about the target job/company before they go along for the interview
- present themselves attractively and intelligently at interview.

Their sales pitch will have been well prepared, focusing not only on what they have to offer but how their talents might benefit the target firm. As part of their homework, they clue up on the firm's history, its current position in the market place and its modus operandi. The result can be very impressive to any employer and gives the applicant a decided advantage over his or her competitors.

Unfortunately, if you have been out of work for some time - or even if you are trying to bail out of a job you hate - your confidence may be at a low ebb when job hunting. You may find you approach job interviews with a sense of desperation... and this attitude shows. After all, you probably *are* desperate. What can you do about it?

There are ways to retrieve your confidence. Feeling genuinely right for the job you're applying for is the most effective way, as you will see.

Before you are ready for the job market, you will need to ascertain the *section* and *level* of the marketplace that is synchronous with your current knowledge and capabilities. If you're aiming for a complete change, you may need new knowledge or further training in preparation.

To make yourself as attractive a commodity as possible, you will also need to 'package' yourself right! If this statement makes you feel like a product rather than a person... well, in a way, you *are* a product when it comes to being selected for a job! You're a commodity that the prospective employer may need and is willing to pay good money for.

Attractive packaging means excellent personal grooming, friendly body language, clear speech and an honest, open manner. It also means an intelligently-formatted and relevant resume!

Well presented and assured of what you can offer in your field of expertise, you will find yourself automatically flowing with confidence...

... because you'll know that you're offering for sale 'quality merchandise': the best of what you ARE and the best of what you DO... to the people who can best USE those capabilities.

THE STARTING POINT

We would like you to regard this book as a map - and your search for *a great job* as an enjoyable and challenging adventure. However, before you can start out on any journey, you need to know where you are right now!

Therefore, to ascertain your starting point, please take some time to fill in the following questionnaire. Give it lots of thought as it will provide you with your current bearings and give you a strong, definitive lead in the right direction.

We have only allotted a line or two per question in order to save space but if you wish, write yourself a whole page or more in response to each answer. Remember, attaining the job of your dreams is the *outcome* you're after… and job search is the *journey*!

WHAT ARE YOU LOOKING FOR IN A JOB?

Be honest; this questionnaire is a self-analysis.
Nobody but you will see the answers.

- **Define what you want in a job:**

  In other words, what do you believe is the right type of job for you?

  _____

  _____

  _____

  _____

  _____

- **Can you pinpoint the job you're after?**

  _____

  _____

  _____

  _____

- **If not, what are the major *components* of the sort of job you are looking for?**

  If you're unable to say exactly what you're after, can you at least identify the *components* of the job you'd like? For example, an accountant with certain strengths like 'people skills' and a love of marketing may recognize that he has these attributes but, at this stage, is not sure of the *job label* that would give him a chance to best use them. If so, he may require professional guidance to assess where that particular mix of strengths would be of greatest value.

  _____

  _____

- **What do you believe are your strengths?**

  _____

  _____

- **What are your weaknesses?**

  _____

  _____

- **Outline your capabilities, trying to be as specific as you can:**

  _____

  _____

- **What limitations do you foresee as being a possible barrier to what you want to do?**

_____

_____

- **Bear in mind that many perceived limitations can be overcome. Could yours? How?**

_____

_____

- **Do you have in mind any particular companies or organisations that you would like to work for - or any idea at this stage where that 'great' job might be?**

_____

_____

- **What attracts you to the above organisations? (e.g. career prospects, image, travel prospects, salary?)**

_____

_____

- **If you have trouble answering the previous 2 questions, can you at least delineate the *type* of company you would like to work for?**

- **What salary are you after?**

- **Is this a realistic figure for your skills on today's market?**

- **Do you have any preferences about location?**

- **Must a car be part of your salary package?**

- **Could you manage without a car, wait for one for a while or afford to provide your own?**

- **Are you prepared to undergo additional training/knowledge acquisition for the new job if necessary?**

- **Do you foresee any hurdles in acquiring further qualifications, education, or skills as you need them?**

  Think about this from every angle. Will you have the money, time, transport, enthusiasm or whatever you need to attain your goal?

- **At this moment, do you feel you possess the right qualifications, education, experience or skills necessary for the type of position you are after?**

- **If not, how could you go about acquiring them?**

- **Would a part-time tertiary, trade or other relevant course assist you at this point in time?**

Often, just the fact that you've started such a course can be a plus. The firm may even offer to pay the course fees if they feel you have potential.

Degrees and diplomas are not always the magic keys to job success. A track record of work experience 'at the coal face' can often be of greater value to an employer; so don't underestimate its worth. Remember, too, that many top businessmen in the past have had only basic elementary education...so don't be overawed by little pieces of paper decorated with wax seals.

- **Have you assessed the influence the following may have on your on your choice of job: salary package, super, share schemes, profit incentive, health fund contributions, insurance for death and disability?**

- **Does the type of job you propose fit your chosen career path?**

If you have just left school or this is your first job, don't be daunted by all those doubts that keep running through your head: 'What if I'm on the wrong career path?' 'What if I don't like this job?' 'What if I wreck my life getting into this?'

You're going to a job, not prison. You will find opportunities to change your career direction at a future date if your subsequent experience in the world shows you that you are better suited to doing something else. Just make as wise a choice as you are capable of at this stage.

The careers counselor at your school, college or university is there to help you assess a viable starting point if you are in doubt. Even if you left school two or three years ago, that ole alma mater will still feel some responsibility toward you and may prove a very important source of information.

So USE it!

NEXT, LET'S DEFINE WHAT YOU *DON'T* WANT IN A JOB!

- **What are (or were) the drawbacks of your current (or previous) job?**

  If possible, identify the *components* and *specifics* of those drawbacks. For example, you may have hated working overtime but was it because it was *UNPAID* overtime or just because you can't stand long working hours?

  _____

  _____

- **What are (or were) the things you think you will miss about it?**

  Don't forget things like camaraderie, commuting time, working hours, travel and other benefits. You are creating an opportunity for a fresh start and will want to avoid previously experienced problems recurring by being alert to the signs and signals that herald them.

  _____

  _____

By now you should have your current bearings and be well equipped to start off in the chosen direction of your journey...

NOW YOU KNOW *WHAT* YOU'RE LOOKING FOR, HOW WILL YOU *FIND* IT?

The first thing you will want to know is what the market-place is currently offering in your line of work…if your old line of work is still worth following up.

The Internet is becoming the most used tool to find jobs these days. In fact, it is not only the preferred job advertising method but can also provide jobseekers with valuable knowledge of companies' backgrounds, recent activities and often, projected goals. But don't ignore magazine and newspaper ads, social media, networking and other groups you may belong to.

Solid preliminary research can arm you with an arsenal of facts that could be vital in showing you have done your homework and are earnest about wanting to work in a particular firm. It may also enable you to assess some of those promises about future pathways that they may make to you.

Many business organisations have their own websites these days and many do their own advertising for jobs. Everyone from small retailers and hobbyists to vast manufacturing concerns and retailers are spending up big in cyberspace as the pressure increases to acquire a real presence in the virtual world.

This way of doing business is pretty hard to escape: it is the way of the moment and of the future… and is progressing in complexity every day (see *Jobs of the Future.* To get just about anywhere now one must be *computer-literate* and if you're not, most libraries can teach you the basics. If you need more than the basics, there are plenty of night schools and on-line courses that can teach you anything else you need.

Examples of popular current sites for job hunters are SEEK, Indeed, CareerBuilder, and LinkedIn. Most are simple to navigate and are broken down into various industries with drop down menus leading to all necessary information such as location, remuneration, job type or function within a particular industry.

Once you have chosen a job ad that you wish to investigate, simply press the 'apply' button. Most ads are designed for immediate application and the facility is generally there for an applicant to attach his or her resume and, for overseas jobs, a visa or work permit.

The Internet has really taken over where job selection ads are concerned and most applicants send in resumes as an email attachment, usually expected to be in Word document format as opposed to a PDF so they can be handled more easily from the recruiter's end.

Should you send a *cover letter*? Generally, it is good idea to send a short, simple summary letter, particularly if you believe that you have something to say that might single yourself out from the crowd - but make it short and succinct.

When will you hear from your prospective employer or recruiter?

The ad itself may provide further information: at the bottom, for example, there may be a line saying something to the effect: '*Please note: only short-listed applicants will be notified*'. In such a case, you can assume that if you are not notified within a reasonable amount of time, you have not been short-listed. If this turns out to be the case, don't despair: *move on*!

After a recruiter and applicant make contact, how does this relationship continue: online, phone, in person, email? This will depend on the level of job you are after. However, generally, with executives, the recruiter will use telephone contact, not only to give you feedback but also to cement a relationship with you. From the recruiter's point of view, even if they have been unsuccessful in landing a good candidate into a job, they will still value building a bridge with that person for the future.

It is good for applicants to have the immediacy of a phone call; it also provides an opportunity for them to ask questions & get a response as well as affording a prime opportunity for continuing negotiation.

The relationship with your recruiter is 2-way: it's important for you to retain some control of what your recruiter is doing on your behalf. You cannot afford to give him or her *carte blanche* to send your resume to everyone. This is a scattergun approach and far from desirable!

You need to ensure that the person representing you is not going to talk to anyone about you unless *you* approve of the contact.

Many candidates send follow-up letters to their recruiter along the lines of *'further to our conversation yesterday, I would like to thank you for representing me to companies X, Y, Z and I look forward to hearing back from you soon'*. This is just a way of re-iterating in black and white the verbal agreement.

How can you ensure your job is handled in a professional way? Answer: by going to a professional recruiter as most candidates' relationships with recruiters are based on trust.

In combing through the various job information sources, it is wise to keep an eye out for any useful information regarding activity in the business world that might affect you: what companies are moving, expanding, opening branches in your area, closing down and so forth. Such information can extend your knowledge of the potential market as well as giving you an insight into the reputation and culture of companies that interest you.

Now... this would probably be as good a place as any to give you some rather surprising news: the majority of people looking for a really *great* job don't find it through advertised selection!

The job market is a bit like an iceberg: only a fraction of it floats above waterline where you can see it. The remainder lies hidden from view, submerged in the depths of... *the Network*!

Read on...

USING 'THE NETWORK'!

What ever is *the Network*? It is an invisible interweaving of people: people who *know* each other, people who *need* each other, people who *use* each other. It is composed of people who *do* things for each other and who pass each other bits of information.

Your network is your list of contacts and your 'help' file all rolled into one. If you don't make yourself part of it, your chance of finding and keeping a *great* job is going to be considerably diminished. If you ever needed *The Network*, you need it now!

If school leavers and first time job seekers think they do not yet have a network, they are mistaken. When they take into account their friends, family members and acquaintances, their relatives' friends... ex-teachers and *social media* contacts... their network is far from non-existent.

So even if you're young and new to networking, pass the word around: "I'm looking for a job!" Every opportunity that you are among people - at parties, discos, weddings, gyms, sports meetings, seminars, holiday tours, hobby courses...or chattering with your millions of friends on *Facebook*...is a chance to increase your network and further increase your chances of learning of job opportunities.

However, social networking has grown up quickly over the past few years and it is so vast that it starting to stratify. Business professionals may use *Facebook* and *Twitter* to while away their pleasurable moments at evenings and the weekend but it is not where *they* would go to search for a '*great*' job. They have their own strata of cyberspace set aside for strictly business, no-nonsense discussion: *LinkedIn* is just one example.

If you wish to enter one of these invisible executive clubs-in-cyberspace to search out job opportunities, you had better know what you want or can realistically offer when you see an appropriate opening. Otherwise, stay out until you do! Unpreparedness and uncertainty in this arena may endow you with a weak, uncertain reputation that may be difficult to eradicate later on. Wishy-washy doesn't cut it around there.

These invisible professional hierarchies needs to be treated with respect for 'you rarely get a second chance to make a first impression' as the saying goes. But *when* you're ready, *if* you're ready, you know the door is there.

Another avenue for leads used by jobseekers of all types is what one might call '*the Clayton's approach*'...as you will see on the next page.

Read more on networking in Part 3,
How To Keep That Great Job!

THE 'CLAYTON'S' APPROACH TO JOBSEEKING

...OR HOW TO ASK FOR A JOB WITHOUT REALLY ASKING FOR A JOB!

How does this work? Very simply - and often very effectively – if you're game! You might ring the company (or companies) you think you would like to work for and ask to speak to the manager of the area that interests you. When you are connected, say that you are wondering if they could suggest someone there who could give you *advice* about entering your field of interest, whatever it might be. If the person to whom you speak is unable to assist you, he or she may suggest someone who can.

When a possible contact is suggested, ring that person. This time, however, you will be in a slightly stronger position than you were before. Why? Because now you have a *referee* of sorts - ie the last person to whom you spoke. You can now try using that referee's name in your introduction: "Oh, hello. My name is XXX. Mr.YYY of ZZZ division suggested I ring you. He thought you might be able to help me. I'm very interested in..."

Remember: you are not asking for a *job* at this stage! You are only asking for some *direction* to the right area or person who may be able to help you. This is a very useful strategy that's worked time and again. Sure, you need a bit of hide...but you also need a job! If the strategy doesn't work on *this* firm, it might work on the *next*...or the next... But you'd be surprised how often it *does* work.

It is also worth ringing a few recruitment consultants, telling them of your specific interests and asking their advice, too. Once again, don't tell them you're 'looking for a job'. After all, so are about twenty thousand other people! Instead, ask for *advice* or *direction*. If they actually invite you to come to see them, they may have a job up their sleeve.

If this search is for your first job, you might say something like (dependent on your background, interests and studies): "I've recently graduated in Human Resources from XXX University and have a Diploma in Chinese from YYY College. I'm interested in finding a challenging HR position in which I could also use my language skills. I'm wondering if you could suggest a likely direction - some firm or organisation - which might be able to help me with such a mix?"

You will find that some consultants specialize in certain job areas while others cover a fairly wide field. If the consultants you ring are unable to assist you themselves, they may give you valuable leads you can follow. On the other hand, they may find you so interesting and so close a match to a job brief they have on their desk right at that moment that they invite you to send in your resume.

Sometimes people need time to think about these types of requests. If they can't think there and then of a likely avenue you could pursue, ask if they would mind your calling them back the next day when they've had time to think it over. People are usually happy to assist you, especially if it is only a simple matter of pointing you in the right direction.

If you are a graduate from a university or college, your own Careers and Appointments area should not be overlooked. Some of the jobs they hear of never reach the general market and might require the very skills you have acquired.

ONE AVENUE YOU MAY NOT HAVE CONSIDERED...

For adventurous young Australians who want a challenging and varied career while receiving top-level education and training but have not quite decided on which discipline they're interested in yet, there is one area on the job front that is often overlooked: the Department of Defence.

The Navy, Army and Air Force offer many exciting opportunities for advancement while instilling leadership, teamwork and interpersonal skills at the highest level. It might be an unusual but highly productive way to put your GAP year to good use by trying out for one of the services while gaining skills, work experience, a good salary, possible travel and friends as well as free medical and dental treatment. The whole job application can be completed online and you should find there most other relevant information you might want.

After applying, you will be asked to attend a Your Opportunities (YOU) session at a Defence Force Recruiting Centre where you will be asked to take a medical test, an Aptitude test and have an interview with a Careers Counsellor. Should you be successful, your next step will be a Medical Assessment to check your physical fitness and you may be asked to perform a few exercises such as sit-ups and push-ups etc. There is also a Psychological Interview to assess whether you are the type of person who would be suited to a military environment and to this end you will be asked quite a few questions about your life to date, employment history, your interests and sporting activities.

Enlistment Day requires another medical check and a welcome ceremony for you and your family... and your military training begins. If you have applied as an officer applicant, there will be extra tests and activities.

Should you have already embarked on a university career and have already completed one year of a three or four year degree – or two years of a five or six year degree - you may be eligible to apply for a Defence University Sponsorship. This means you could receive a salary while you are studying, with your HELP debt reduced and remaining fees paid, super contribution, subsidised accommodation, free medical and dental care as well as a career where you can gain respect and really make a difference in the world at an early age.

Read all about the job opportunities including spending your GAP year in the ADF on the ADF Education site: http://www.defencejobs.gov.au/education/

PREPARING YOUR RESUME...

Your resume - in other words, your CV (curriculum vitae) - is just what its name suggests: a resume or summary of your educational and on-the-job experience that generally shows some relevance to the particular job for which you're applying.

That document is your 'bait' for catching the initial interest of recruiters or prospective employers. In fact, in the early stages of job selection, it will be the only intimation they have of you... and what you can offer them. For this reason, what you write needs to be well formatted and well-worded: short, sharp and simple.

If this is your first job and you are uncertain about how your information should be laid out, you may wish to follow the *Do-It-Yourself Resume Guide* included at the back of this manual. Alternatively, if you prefer to have your resume prepared professionally, look for a consultant under 'Resumes' or 'Employment' on the web or in the classified ads of your local newspaper or even in the *Yellow Pages*.

Your resume - a truthful, concise reflection of your educational and career experience to date - should not exceed three or four pages unless you are in a very senior position with a long and relevant career history. Then it could run to many pages.

You are expected to give no more than a very brief outline of your work history, highlighting responsibilities held and achievements gained in each *major* job you have had.

If you have had a string of jobs, don't try cramming details of all of them into your resume; it is most unlikely that many of them would be relevant to the job in question.

Nevertheless, if there is a period of your life that involved you in many short-term jobs - and you wish to refer to that - do so in a general way. For example, let's assume that way back in the 1990's you spent three years on the road with the circus and two more with a rock band: under normal circumstances, you might simply refer to that period as: 'five years experience in the entertainment industry'. On the other hand, if the job you're chasing is actually *in* the entertainment industry, that experience would assume greater relevance and would deserve to be detailed.

In other words, focus the content of your resume around those details that will show you in the best light for this particular job, concentrating on your most *recent* or most *relevant* career experience.

Unfortunately, that resume of yours - so lovingly and thoughtfully put together - is likely to be just one of dozens received by the recruiter or prospective employer for the same position you're after. What will single *yours* out of the crowd?

Unless you have some 'one-in-a-million' skill that they just happen to be looking for (which leaves them no choice but to hire you!), you're going to have to find a way of 'selling yourself' to them initially via this one document and the covering letter that goes with it.

To do this, your resume will need to be outstanding in presentation and layout, giving the impression that you are logical, self-disciplined, organized and can express yourself well.

It should also be positive in tone, emphasizing your achievements rather than just listing duties and responsibilities you've had. Better still, always try to *quantify* your achievements in percentages or numbers, where possible.

You need to grab the reader's attention by what you say on the first couple of pages...so use these to advantage. One good ploy is to put a short Career Profile right up on the front page (as in the *D.I.Y. Resume Guide* examples). This sums you up, saying: "This is me in a nutshell!"

Notice, too, that your career history should be listed in *reverse chronological order*, from your most recent job backwards. Do the same thing with your educational details: put tertiary or higher education first and secondary education last - if at all. (Again, refer to the examples we've given in the *D.I.Y. Resume Guide* at the end of the book.)

If you are not sending in an digtal copy of your resume, a photocopy is generally acceptable providing it is clear to read and spotless. Hard copies should look as though they have just come off a laser printer.... clean, smooth and never dog-eared! Send it with its covering letter in an A4 envelope, so there will be no need to fold it.

A few hints on style:

- Use a series of bullet points laid out in the manner of these paragraphs. (The actual bullet symbol '•' itself is not strictly necessary but is usually accomplished through by holding the option key & pressing number 8; alternatively you could use asterisks).

- Isolate each career highlight, achievement and responsibility etc. This means space will be limited...so you will need to be selective in what you say.

- 10-point text allows you to fit more into the two-column format without appearing cramped. However, much depends on the font you choose. Fonts can vary in height and width so you will need to experiment.

- Use **BOLD, UPPER CASE & <u>UNDERLINED</u>** type for main headings and for the name of the company or firm you worked in.

- Use **bold, lower case** type for subheadings.

- Write a short **CAREER PROFILE** or a summation of your **CAREER OBJECTIVES** on the first page so the reader can see at a glance who you are and what you are about.

- Be sure to list the various positions you've held in **REVERSE CHRONOLOGICAL ORDER,** with emphasis on your most **RECENT** jobs.

The *D.I.Y. Resume Guide* at the back of this manual will show you an easy, simple way of formatting your information if you are an absolute beginner

When job hunting, you will probably need to make changes in your resume from time to time to appear more relevant for specific jobs. This will necessitate emphasizing certain achievements you have gained in the past. Give this careful thought.

If your resume looks poorly formatted, grubby and unprofessional, with poor grammar and spelling, it could quickly end up in the recruiter's 'slush pile' of doubtful contenders. This would be a pity, particularly if you were actually perfect for the job. Don't let this happen to you when you can avoid it! Some job ads elicit such a huge mail response that you can't afford to take a chance with a second-rate resume presentation.

Of course, we cannot say that there are no exceptions to all these rules. There have been times where people who were passed over during the initial desk assessment have finally ended up with the job! But it's unusual.

Make it easy on yourself! Get a head start by presenting an immaculate, impressive and relevant resume.

Don't give your competitors an advantage!

THE COVERING LETTER

A resume alone is unlikely to sell you, though it will help. There are often dozens of people applying for any advertised job; therefore, you will need something to single *your* resume out of the crowd.

This is the purpose of the covering letter: to persuade the reader you should be interviewed. It accompanies your resume and should never be omitted. As it represents YOU, it should also be well expressed and to-the-point, occupying as short a space as possible.

In it, you will need to give a very brief summary of your main experience and skills and *how they relate to the particular job* for which you're applying. Although only a few paragraphs long, this letter must be the best bit of self-selling you have ever done.

You may think that sending a covering letter is over-kill considering you've put all the necessary details in the resume. Far from it! This letter will give you a 'face'. It introduces you as a *personality* rather than a mere summation of facts.

Always be specific about the job you're applying for as the firm may have several others going as well. Refer to the job title (e.g. 'Sales Manager - Retail') and the source of your information (e.g. ' as advertised in *THE AGE*, August 16th, 2027')!

(If you are uncertain of the format, content or tone of your covering letter, it would be worth taking your draft to a Careers Counsellor for critical discussion.)

Clear, easy-to-read and professionally-typed copy is always preferable. Use simple, straight-forward language without any errors in spelling or grammar. Keep it to one page, if posssible, and if it is not being sent by email, place it - covering your resume - in an appropriately-sized envelope so neither document has to be folded or creased.

The letter should present you as a mature, intelligent individual and draw attention to those aspects of your experience or interest that you believe make you appropriate and adaptable for the job. If you already know the name of the company offering the job, show you are acquainted with the organization, its objectives or products in what you say. Then offer yourself for interview.

***Think of the covering letter as a smile and
a handshake in an envelope!***

JOB APPLICATION FORMS

A job advertisement may invite you to send for an application form in the first instance. When you receive it, read it thoroughly then practice writing your answers to each of the questions on a piece of scrap paper until you are satisfied with your responses. Perfect them then copy them clearly and neatly onto the form.

Answer all the questions honestly. If you can't answer a certain question or you feel something does not relate to you, explain why briefly. If there is insufficient room in the allotted space, put an asterisk with 'see below' next to it; then write your brief explanation beside another asterisk at the foot of the form. Don't just leave questions unanswered.,

Write a short COVERING LETTER to accompany the form.

LETTERS OF INTRODUCTION

If you are writing a letter of introduction to enquire whether an organisation or agency has any available positions, do try to be specific about the sort of job you'd like. If you take a general 'I'll-do-anything' approach, you may devalue yourself in the reader's eyes.

Think about what you, specifically, could offer such an organisation in the way of your present capabilities, experience, knowledge, strengths and potential. Mention anything about yourself that could be of special interest to the employer.

Consider what the firm could offer *you*. What draws you to *it*? What have you heard or read about it?

For example:

'Dear (name of relevant person in firm),

I am most impressed by the achievements of your firm in .... *(mention a particular area)*, an area in which I have a particular interest.

I would love to have an opportunity to speak with you about.............etc.'

Then, offer yourself for interview.

DON'T FORGET TO ATTACH YOUR RESUME!

JOB HUNTING... IF YOU ARE CURRENTLY EMPLOYED

(WHOA! DON'T QUIT YOUR OLD JOB YET... UNLESS YOU'RE REALLY DESPERATE!)

It's a good idea to hang on to your old job until you are offered the new one - providing staying on is not too stressful! Generally, you appear more substantial to a prospective employer or recruiter if you are currently employed - even if the job you are in is totally irrelevant to the one you're applying for. It creates the impression that you have proved to be a satisfactory employee...and that you don't give up easily!

Secondly, from your own point of view, just the knowledge that you have a weekly wage coming in will make you less vulnerable to an unsuitable offer from a work culture you know intuitively you're going to hate. (After all you're after a '*great*' job, remember?)

Being employed means you will be bargaining from a position of strength. Even some form of temporary work will help give you 'staying power' and more self-confidence in your job search.

However, a lot depends on the type of position you're in. If your current job entails very long hours, for example, it may be difficult for you to arrange time out for job interviews. In such a case, it would be best for you to free yourself from the shackles of the unsatisfactory position and do your job-hunting unencumbered.

Danger: Best not to talk about your job-hunting manoeuvres or interview appointments to friends on social media! You never know who knows who!

JOB HUNTING... IF YOU
ARE UNEMPLOYED

The pangs of hunger often breed a sense of desperation in those who have rent to pay, a family to support - but no income. Unless you are a good actor, that desperation can make you over-anxious; not a viable emotion in job search. What can you do?

As we have seen in an earlier chapter, some people have been unemployed for so long, they start to feel incompetent and their self-esteem goes out the window.

For this reason, as well as for the financial benefits, it is wise to consider trying to find small interim jobs while you're looking around. There is always some service-oriented work available - like gardening, lawn-mowing, dog-walking or pet-feeding for absent owners, delivering pizzas, baby sitting or house cleaning.

If there is nothing suitable advertised, you might consider devising your own small ad for the internet job sites or the newspaper classifieds...or even making up some leaflets for distribution in your neighbourhood.

Even if you were to fill in with some interim service jobs like dog walking or babysitting, they will not only help keep the wolf from the door; they will help to keep up your people skills, your self-confidence and self esteem.

And who knows where such seemingly 'menial' tasks may lead? There are millionaires out there who have built huge businesses from doing such work. (We'll talk more about this later in the chapter entitled *Jobs of the Future*.)

Alternatively, the personnel agencies usually have a variety of temporary or contract work on their books which could give you the opportunity to try out a range of different jobs. You may even find one that will lead you to permanent employment.

Perhaps you are not in any dire need and are well able to support yourself while you look for a job. You know what you want - and feel all you're waiting for is the 'big break'.

You can MAKE that 'big break' happen whenever you're ready...
by following this guide and putting yourself into ACTION!

MANAGING TIME EFFECTIVELY

If you are currently jobless and at home, it is easy to mismanage or waste your time. You could find yourself staying in bed later and later each morning and, when you do get up, you may put a thousand inconsequential things before your all-important job search activities. Procrastination and disorganisation can kill success before it starts: relentless determination, self-organisation and planning help create it.

The unemployed should realise right here and now that they already have a job: their job is... to find themselves a job!

Sure, you may not get paid a weekly wage for scouring the job market and writing all those letters, but you will be paid in terms of future job satisfaction and financial security if you go about it the right way. So accept the fact that you have employed *yourself* to find a really great job - and if you succeed, you will get the profit!

If you are currently unemployed, one of the most effective things you can do to keep yourself from going 'stale' and keep your job-hunting interest alive is to make yourself a time management sheet for the kitchen wall.

Firstly, work out how many hours per day you will spend on your job search, taking into account the various methods available to you.

Next, make a list of the companies and organisations which you believe might value your skills and knowledge and that you feel might be worth contacting. You may find it helpful to buy an indexed notebook for this purpose.

In your notebook, write the name of each organisation that interests you -and why - and against the organisation's name jot down a few details: whether you saw their web or magazine advert or if they were referred to you by someone… or you merely discovered them through hearsay. Note the names or titles of the people to whom you might speak - either on the phone or in person as well as deadline dates and other requirements. Leave plenty of space to write any subsequent feedback you get from contacting them.

Next turn to searching for job sites on the Internet – there are many. *Seek* and *Indeed* are examples of popular ones at the moment as we have mentioned but business professionals are more likely to do their searching on sites like *LinkedIn*. Depending on the type of job you are after, you might also spend a few hours searching out relevant job ads in the backs of specialist or academic magazines at the library or the news agency.

You will also need time to work on your resume. Even if you have one already prepared, you will need to tailor it to whatever job you're applying for and create an appropriate covering letter.

Pinning time management schedules to your wall and keeping an indexed notebook for your job search contacts will assist you greatly in organising yourself. So, too, will a special-purpose diary for jotting down those all-important appointments and interviews.

LANDING AN INTERVIEW

Job-hunting can actually be quite enjoyable and informative - or it can be stressful, dreary and disheartening. It depends how you approach it.

Above all, you need to be realistic about your abilities and qualifications. If they are minimal, think about the old saying: *'It's better to be a large fish in a small pond than a small fish in a large pond.'* Make it big in the small pond first - then swim up a level or two as you build a reputation for yourself.

Make job-hunting a game, a challenge. It seems that everything that happens in life has an average success rate, from hitting a cricket ball to being struck by lightning. Think of this when you're knocking on doors, writing job applications and ringing for interviews.

In those initial stages of the job search, think of looking for a job as if you were finding out your individual 'batting average'…i.e.in landing a likely interview. Is it one out of ten, twenty or fifty calls tries? It has to be one out of something. That's Nature Law of Numbers!!!

Go play the game! All you need to do is find your score!

It's easy to be negative about knock-backs. It's easier still to ensure that you don't get any at all - by doing nothing! But by doing nothing, you'll end up with nothing! So play the game and focus on *winning*! That way, even if your batting average turns out to be one out of a hundred, what does it matter? All you're after is one 'yes' to give you confidence!

If you're sourcing jobs, apply as the ad suggests. Only an address or P.O. box number may have been revealed at this initial stage - or there may be a phone number. If there is an invitation to ring, do so and find out all you can about the position. You may feel nervous about ringing; if so, write down the questions you want to ask beforehand - in case you go blank.

In fact, it is not a bad idea to have the self-questionnaire from our manual to hand, even though you've practiced the answers a hundred times. That way, if the recruiter asks you a curly question, you'll never be at a loss for words! Recruiters often make an initial assessment over the telephone, particularly for jobs where good communication skills are important.

When phoning firms, try to avoid lunchtime.

If you catch a person just about to go to lunch, he or she may be too rushed or just too plain hungry to give you the hearing you deserve.

It is unlikely your phone call will elicit the name of the actual firm offering the job - unless they are doing their own recruiting. You may not even be told where the job is other than: "in the CBD" or "in the Eastern suburbs". Don't pressure the recruiter to be specific at this stage; it will only antagonise. You'll find out everything you need to know at interview.

If dollars haven't been mentioned in the ad and you feel you simply *must* have an idea of the salary range (and 'range only' is probably all you'll ever be told at this stage) to help you to decide whether the job's worth applying for, you could ask...'what sort of salary package are you offering?' However, don't dwell on salary at this point: you want them to think you're more interested in job satisfaction than dollars.

If you are perceived as being relevant, you will be asked to send in a copy of your resume. For this reason, it is best to have a basic C.V already prepared before you begin job-hunting, then simply tailor it to each job you apply for. You will need to write that short, well-worded covering letter to accompany the resume as well. This, too, will be specific to each job and may take a while to draft.

If there is no contact phone number offered, just send off your resume and covering letter directly to the address offered in the manner requested and wait for a reply... fingers crossed!

ARRANGING INTERVIEWS WHILE YOU ARE STILL EMPLOYED

You should go about your job hunting with the stealth and cunning of a CIA agent. Try to organise after-work or early morning interviews if possible so nobody at your current workplace will be suspicious.

And don't make calls to prospective employers from your office phone if you are likely to be overheard. You are far safer using a mobile phone in order to keep your nefarious appointment-making private.

If you are still employed, it is best not to discuss your job plans or talk about interviews with *anyone* yet... especially on social media! This is a hard task. It is only human to want to discuss with friends and colleagues the pros and cons of your career path - but it's also very dangerous.

You would be surprised by who knows who - and how well people can put two and two together, regardless of the level of employment you are in. Your best buddy may just happen to mention to another buddy that you're looking at job vacancies and before you know it, the office 'grapevine' will have spread the news like magic.

PREPARING FOR THE INTERVIEW

'Doing your homework' is essential if you are to get the edge on your competitors in an interview. Going to an interview well-informed is not only a courtesy but will give you loads of confidence, enable you to understand comments and ask intelligent questions.

You can ring and ask the company and ask if they have a *job description* or further information they could send you about the position you are applying for. They are more likely to accede to this request if you already have an interview lined up - but it's worth asking anyway. Firms vary widely on giving out a job description beforehand; sometimes they prefer to reserve it for the interview itself and have you read it in the interview room.

Hopefully, your own background research on the firm will throw up such useful facts as its size, growth rate, range of services and so forth.

Also, if you have any trustworthy contacts who are already in the organisation, they may be able to fill you in on the firm's history, policies and general philosophy. (However, beware that your informant's 'facts' are not tainted by office politics.)

There is little that Google will not sniff out for you but there are other avenues for those who are not au fait with the wonders of the electronic world. *The Business Who's Who?* at your local library may yield further information on the firm if it is a major one, as could many others like *Jobson's Year Book of Public Companies*, *The U.B.D.*, *The Stock Exchange Handbook* and *Kompass Australia*. Skim for articles relating to a firm's recent history in business magazines and journals too. Librarians are always delighted to help.

However, The Internet will usually yield a wealth of recent information on major companies and it can be accessed at most major libraries if you do not have your own on-line capability.

THE DAY OF THE INTERVIEW

Be sure to arrive at the appointed time, preferably earlier. Being late rings warning bells with consultants *and* prospective employers. Not only might they be irate feeling they've had to waste their valuable time in waiting for you but they could get the impression that you're disorganised and could turn up late on the job each day.

KNOW YOUR INTERVIEWERS

You will either be invited to see a recruiter or, if the firm is doing its own recruiting, to apply direct.

There can be quite a difference in attitude between recruitment consultants and prospective employers when it comes to hiring personnel. A recruitment consultant's hope is to make money out of a placement, so the emphasis is on making *you* (if you're relevant to the position) look as good as possible to the employer.

Employers, on the other hand, may be more concerned with how candidates are going to make *them* look. Applicants need to take into account the possibility of self-interest that may exist in various situations.

It will help you if you know beforehand whether your up-coming interview is to be on a one-to-one basis or before a panel. Maybe you could ask the secretary this question so you can be mentally prepared! For some people, it can be quite disconcerting to have to face multiple questioners all at once. However, there is little you can do about it if that is how the interview is structured.

If you have prepared yourself as this manual suggests, you should have no problem coping with the questions and answers...but you need to remember to adjust your attention and body language to encompass *everyone* there if you are presenting before a panel.

Don't keep your gaze fixed on the kindliest-looking or
most sympathetic face whilst ignoring the others!

Everybody likes to feel important and included in any group context - and this goes for your interviewers as well. So make the effort to warm to them and they will warm to you.

Remember each person sitting before you is a human being. They might look important on the other side of the table - but be assured that under those neat ties and scarf pins, they all harbor fears, worries, hopes and dreams just like you. All of them - even the MD - wants to be successful, looked up to, loved and respected just as you do.

So give the whole panel your attention: direct what you have to say to each person using eye-to-eye contact, empathy…and smile occasionally. And give handshakes all round when you enter and leave.

OVERCOMING NERVOUSNESS

Instead of focusing on whether *you* are making a good impression on the interviewer and what they might be thinking of you, concentrate instead on *what's being discussed.* Immerse yourself in it entirely. You'll soon be so wrapped up in the conversation that you'll forget about yourself and your nerves will disappear as if by magic.

Clear, *two-way communication* should be your number one priority.

Try not to go in with the attitude of a beggar: "I wonder if I will get this job? I wonder if they will *like* me? I wonder what they are thinking of me?"

Instead, concentrate on *them*! Be mindful of what contribution you think you could make because of your special strengths, your experience, your values and work ethic. Think: what could you do for *them?*

SELF-focus makes you SELF-conscious!

Here's a helpful tip from an actor who found a way to get over his nervousness before going on-stage: "Before the performance, squeeze, hold, then relax each part of your body… from your toes up through the various parts of your body to your face. Then concentrate totally on your deep breath: inhale for 5 counts - hold - then exhale for 5 counts, slowly and deeply."

Finally, a good stretch and yawn does wonders for nerves, too...
but only if you can do it without being seen!

PERSONAL PRESENTATION

To *be* a success, you need to *look* a success! But how can you look a success if you are jobless and your bank account is zero?

To start with, your interviewers don't know this! With the right preparation, what they will see before them is a client who is beautifully groomed: polished shoes, ironed clothes, dandruff-free shoulders, washed hair, clean collar and cuffs and perfectly tied tie. Attention to these details, besides making you look professional and at your polished best, will go a long way to giving you inner confidence and pride.

Candidates who thoughtlessly eat garlic or onions or drink alcohol before an interview are virtually saying, "don't give the job to *me*! I'm not a team person. I only care about *myself*!" As for smoking or chewing during an interview: no!no!no!

It's important to dress appropriately for the *level* of job for which you are applying. A well-tailored and immaculately pressed suit is generally the safest bet for either sex in a professional position. It is better to look a bit overdressed than underdressed, especially in a corporate interview.

On the other hand, if you are applying for a job as a laborer, clean well-pressed casual clothes will be more in keeping.

Professional 'image consultants' charge big dollars for such advice in image-enhancement seminars. However, plain commonsense preparation of grooming, neat dress and mindful body language can give you the same result.

In fact, body language is extremely important: as we said earlier - shake hands firmly while you look your interviewer in the eyes... and *smile warmly*. Sit comfortably in the chair they offer you but *not* until asked. Sit normally in the chair: if you slump back in the seat, you'll give the impression that you're slack, not just relaxed. If you perch on the edge of the seat like a bird ready to fly, you'll appear nervous or highly strung.

There are certain other traits which irritate interviewers like overbearing, aggressive behavior or a cocky 'I'm-the-greatest' attitude. There is never any need for this. Instead, be authentic and earnest in what you say, smile, look your interviewer in the eyes when you speak - and speak clearly.

Like everybody else in the world, interviewers love to hear their own names. Referring to them as 'er... Mr. um...' or 'ah...' suggests you find them of little importance. Just imagine how *you* would feel if the interviewer opened the door and said to you, "Come in, er... um... and sit down!'

Find out their names beforehand from the secretary if you are not sure. Ensure too that you have the correct pronunciation. Embarrassing blunders have been made in the past with unfamiliar or foreign names!

And - dare we say it again? - even if you are knocking at the knees, remember: *SMILE* and be empathetic, especially when you arrive and leave.

All this easier said than done? Not if you have prepared well.

Preparation gives confidence; TONS of
preparation gives TONS of confidence!

THE INTERVIEW

Your recruiters want you to talk to them; why would you be there otherwise? So be prepared to communicate! Give - and ASK for - information, in your nicest and most vivacious way. They will want to know about you just as you want to know about them, so regard the interview as an 'exchange of information' and 'mutual assessment'.

Unfortunately, candidates who look good on paper sometimes do not fulfill expectations when they present in person. Certain qualities in addition to the specified qualifications may be required; things such as a sense of maturity, creative thinking, ability to grasp concepts quickly, an eye for detail, excellent grooming, clear diction - or a thousand-and-one-other possibilities, depending on the position.

All the time, your interviewers will be trying to establish what your REAL strengths and abilities are. You could have a wad of documents extolling your virtues and skills but these don't always tell the full story about you. There have even been occasions where documents such as degrees and certificates have been forged.

Mostly, however, they will be trying to assess whether you will 'fit' snugly into their culture and the vacancy that exists in it. Every job has its own specific requirements. For example, leadership qualities may be valued in one job but they may be a drawback in another.

Where leadership is required, recruiters will generally look for qualities of intelligence, maturity and good interpersonal skills. They won't want someone who is pushy or tyrannical but a person who shows evidence of understanding the needs and wants of others.

Successful leaders generally lead by example. They seem to have an inbuilt, intuitive grasp of situations as they arise, and are able to convince and enthuse others about their plans and ideas. They listen to and show respect for their followers' suggestions and ideas, too - even if they don't use them. A good leader is able to unify the members of his or her team, imbuing them with a sense of self-worth and dedication and inducing them to carry out necessary company plans faithfully and with commitment.

Sometimes people in managerial positions suffer from feelings of stress and inadequacy believing it is incumbent on them to show they are born leaders capable of performing workplace wonders.

Admittedly managers need to be gifted organisers and intelligent administrators with above-average interpersonal skills - but their position is really one of 'team coach' whose main purpose is to blend a group of different individuals into a smoothly running, success-oriented machine and then be able to maintain it well.

Managers who happen to be good leaders as

well are pure gold to any organisation!

QUESTIONS YOU'RE LIKELY TO BE ASKED

In answering your interviewers, we advocate that you try to be honest and to the point. There are some image consultants preparing jobseekers for interview who take quite a different approach to this. They suggest candidates approach the interview as actors would approach a stage and that they give their 'audience' (viz. their interviewers) only the story that they think will get them the job, truthful or not.

In many cases, this approach works: the applicants get the job by using dishonesty. But the question is: will they manage to *keep* the job? With some positions, there is an initial trial period of three months or so. When that period is up, will it become apparent that these people were all talk and no substance - and will they soon find themselves back on the same job hunting adventure? It is very likely they will: but, this time, they will be hunting around with a black mark against their name. It will be uncomfortable indeed at the next interview to answer such questions as: "What was your last job? Why did you leave so soon after starting?"

So, 'intelligent honesty' is by far the best policy...especially considering you'll be reference-checked before getting the next job. A bit of 'tailoring' of yourself to the position will never go astray but you need to be confident that you can follow through if you *do* get the job.

You will also be assessed on such things as your apparent enthusiasm, motivation, tenacity, team spirit, work preferences, how you cope with challenges etc.

Interviewers have a tendency to ask 'open-ended' questions to encourage the candidate to talk. However, even if you are asked 'closed questions' (i.e. questions that seem to require only yes/no answers), don't feel hesitant about responding as fully as you can.

Candidates should practice answering the following questions on a *voice-recorder* then listen critically to *play-back*. Do you sound as though you know what you're talking about? Are you lucid, self-confident, modest yet convincing?

In interview, listen carefully to the questions you are being asked and think before you speak. It's pointless learning your answers off-by-heart, parrot fashion, because questions may be framed in all sorts of unexpected ways. However, if you've had a lot of practice thinking about such questions and using that tape recorder till the tape is worn, you will have no trouble fashioning appropriate responses. Practice until your answers convince *you*!

Here are some of the types of questions you're sure to be asked... although your interviewers will probably phrase them differently. If you've been for previous job interviews, you will already be aware of such key questions that keep coming up.

KEY QUESTIONS

- **Why would you like to work for our company or organisation?**

  You will have an impressive answer ready here because you will have done your homework on what this particular firm can offer you... and you will have related it to what you want. This will show that you *know* what you want and how to *get* it.

  Don't forget to incorporate into the conversation your well-researched knowledge of their products and/or services and the relevance of those products/services to your interests or aims.

  _____

  _____

  _____

- **Tell us about your career to date.**

  Yes, it's all there on your CV, but they'll want to hear it from your own lips. Tell them the *highlights* of your career, the success stories. Throw in facts and figures to substantiate. (However, always tell your wondrous history with a modest demeanor, letting the facts themselves speak for your ability.)

  _____

  _____

  _____

- **What was your greatest achievement or challenge in your last job as far as the organisation was concerned?**

- **What were your performance appraisals like in your last position?**

- **Why did you leave your last job?**

Be careful here! Never *trash* your previous employers or workmates even if you boil every time you think of them!

Even if some truly intolerable situation or relationship caused you to leave your last job, you'll need to find a positive way of explaining it. Try to make your resignation or sacking the fault of a *situation*, not the fault of a *person*.

For example, if you left because you found it boring and repetitive, it would be preferable to say something like: "it didn't offer me the sort of challenges I'm looking for". This then shows you up in a positive light as a person who likes challenges!

If you left because of some difficult person or persons, your tack would be to say something along the lines of: "I felt my talents were not being utilised (or recognised)" or "I felt there was little opportunity for advancement for me there."

If you were retrenched, say so. It's a daily occurrence these days so don't say it with shame. Talk about the SITUATION that led to your being asked to go (clever technology that maybe led to downsizing or a take-over by another big firm etc). Don't give the impression you're a nervous wreck because of it. Let them see that you are quite confident about getting another job and are actually looking forward to new experiences and challenges.

- ## Where do you hope to go in your career?

Goal-oriented people will have this one already worked out in a series of well-laid-out steps. They will know where they want to be in two years, five years, ten years from now.

A mere shrug and a passive wishy-washy answer like 'I don't know' would indicate lack of planning and direction.

Show *you* are a goal-oriented person with a clear career objective!

- ## What are your aims and aspirations?

Don't say things like 'I want to have my own business one day' - even if you do! A genie is not asking you to make three wishes; you are being assessed as to whether you will be a productive cog in the machinery of the firm right now...*and* if you will continue to be of use to them after they have poured their money and expertise into you over the next few years.

- **What is likely to afford you job satisfaction?**

  Hint: Don't say 'money'! Don't mention material possessions! Keep it CAREER-ORIENTED all the way.

- **What would you say are your strengths?**

- **What do you feel are your weaknesses?**

  Aren't you glad you practised your answers to these two questions over and over with that tape recorder?

- **Of the jobs you have held in the past, which did you enjoy the most? Why?**

_____

_____

_____

- **What are some of your interests and hobbies? What type of books do you read?**

  You may have lots of hobbies and interests but this is not the time or place to list them all. Mention only the main ones, otherwise you could look like a scatterbrain.

_____

_____

_____

- **What made you choose this line of work or study? Did you go into it for want of something better to do...or did you choose it because you really liked it?**

  Your answer here could reveal feelings from apathy to obsession. Hopefully, it will indicate genuine interest.

_____

_____

- **Have you had any previous experience in this type of work?**

  If you've only recently left school, any work experience you've had in this area will lend weight to your evinced interest in the job.

- **Are you willing to do more menial tasks if it's part of the position?**

  This could involve anything - tea and coffee making, going to the bank, driving miles to deliver some article or report.

- **Of what value has your previous work experience been to you?**

  No matter what you've done before, even if it seems totally unrelated, it usually can be shown to have some relevance to the job you're applying for if you think hard about it. But the time to fashion your answer is well before the interview. How has your work experience helped you? What use could it have to this job? Did it instil discipline, improve your organisational skills, team leadership etc?

- **What are the most important considerations for you in choosing a job?**

  If you answer 'salary', 'really nice office', 'one way to get a 'late model car', 'better working hours' or any other trite reason, go straight to jail, do not pass 'Go' and do not collect $200! What they are trying to elicit from you is your interest and enthusiasm for the job itself. What do you think you can do for the company? What do you hope to get out of it in satisfaction and prospects for the future?

- **Have you done - or are you doing - any further study to assist you achieve your aim in this line of work?**

  A positive answer will suggest not only genuine interest but self-motivation and dedication. Your study performance - ie your results at school or University - are often regarded as an indicator of how you may perform at work. If your results were poor, you'd better be ready with some good excuse: for example, 'I am determined not to let this happen again'.

Applicants will face many other questions that will be JOB-SPECIFIC and this manual cannot possibly predict nor list all of them. For example, an applicant presenting for a job in a local fish and chip shop will be asked quite different questions to one presenting for the position of accountant in a fish processing firm. The preceding pages list the general questions that you are likely to be asked regardless of the type of job you are going for. If you have those answers down pat - and spend adequate preparation time before your interview thinking up and answering more *specific* questions that you think likely, you will have very little trouble convincing your interviewers that you are a worthy contender for the job.

QUESTIONS *YOU* CAN ASK THEM!

Don't be afraid to ask a few questions of your own. They'll appreciate your intelligent interest. After all, you need to know what you're getting yourself into. Depending on the level and type of job you are going for, you might ask for information on such things as:

- **Job direction:** (that is, where the job is likely to take you - if anywhere.)
- **What training programs are available, either now or in the future.**
- **The reason the job vacancy exists:** (if you don't find this out, YOU might end up vacating the job for the same reason as your predecessor!)
- **The company's plans for the future:** (information regarding its expected growth, mobility etc.)

  Then ask yourself: *'Will I be happy and stimulated working among these people? Is this my scene?'*

CAUTION: A COUPLE OF DON'T'S...

RE SALARY:

Don't appear too anxious about salary. In the initial interview, your immediate focus should be the job, what you think you can do for the firm and what you hope it will do for you.

If, during or after a subsequent interview, you are offered the job - but believe you're worth more than they want to pay you - you could try negotiating: e.g. request they reconsider the salary package in view of your level of past experience etc. If they ask you to nominate what you think you are worth, you'll have to come up with a very realistic figure!

Alternatively, it may be possible to offer your services at the going price for a limited time - say six months - with a salary review after you've proved your worth.

RE OFFICE POLITICS:

Whatever you do, don't let your foot get caught on the sticky floor of office politics. Your research of the firm and its problems may have led you to a source of gossip and backbiting. Keep this information to yourself and just be wary where you tread.

WHEN YOUR INTERVIEW
IS OVER...

Thank your interviewers for their time and, if you think you would like to be considered for the position, LET THEM KNOW of your interest.

Ask if there is to be another interview for short-listed candidates; if the answer is yes, indicate you hope to be invited and ask how long before they are able to let you know.

In the unlikely - but possible - event that you are offered the job before you leave, don't dilly-dally with your answer IF you're sure you want it. Say 'yes' there and then if possible. If you're unable to do this because you need time to think it over, explain this situation to them honestly and politely - but leave no one in doubt about your interest.

Tell them *when* you will give them your answer - 'in the morning' or 'by 5 pm tomorrow'. (Don't ask them to wait too long; there are plenty of other fish in the sea!)

When leaving, remember to smile and say thank you to each of your interviewers, not forgetting to say each person's name as you confidently shake his or her hand.

PSYCHOLOGICAL TESTING

Firms are divided on psychological tests. Some feel it is necessary to assess aptitude for certain positions: others say that if they can't recruit without personality testing, they don't know much about their business.

It seems that those firms which do use psychological tests are convinced of their efficacy, so don't fight 'em! Just go along and do your best!

Here are a few points that might be of help in such a test:

- It is a good idea to look for books on psych testing, General Intelligence (IQ) tests and Emotional Intelligence (EQ) tests from the library or download examples from the Internet. One old but much-used test is the Myers Briggs Personality Test which can be practiced on-line for free: some websites offer a full career report with theirs. However, there are many types of tests these days including numerical and verbal reasoning skills, aptitude tests and so forth and it will be well worth your time to research them so you will be prepared.

- By practicing sample tests of varying kinds, you will soon get the hang of the type of questions asked. Many psychometric tests consist of a number of interdependent and interconnecting questions scattered throughout the paper; your answers will not necessarily be 'right' or 'wrong' but they will show up some of your major tendencies. One set of questions may be out to assess your sociability, another your team spirit, resilience, leadership ability and so forth.

- When you are given the test, you will also be given a time in which to complete it. Don't panic. To help you calm down, answer the *easy* questions first. This will not only save you time; it will give you greater confidence and get you into the 'mood' of the test. You may even find yourself quite enjoying it! Then go back if you can and try to answer the easier of the questions that are left. Last of all, attempt the more difficult ones.

IF YOU'VE BEEN WAITING FOR DAYS - BUT NO FEEDBACK!

Ring them! If you were originally referred or interviewed by a consultant ring the CONSULTANT. If you applied to the company direct, ring the COMPANY. (But *don't*, under *any* circumstances, ring the *company* if you have been dealing with a consultant!)

Tell your contact you are extremely interested in the position and hope they don't mind your ringing...but you would just like some feedback if possible on how your application is going.

Always be polite and smile while you're talking: yes, even on the phone! It takes the anxiety out of your voice - and the warmth it creates will be picked up by the person at the other end. Accept whatever they tell you and don't push your luck.

IF, AFTER ALL THE PREPARATION, YOU WEREN'T INVITED FOR INTERVIEW

Such a situation is no reflection on *you*. After all, the firm didn't even see you! Get back on the path and start looking for something more suitable right away!

Your qualifications or work history may not have been perceived as being sufficiently relevant for *this* particular job - but there is a job out there that's right for you. All you've got to do is find it.

Remember, as we said at the beginning, in knocking on doors and sending in resumes, you're discovering your hit rate! Everyone has one... including *you*.

Keep in mind the well-used NLP supposition:
'there's no failure, only feedback!'

IF YOU WERE INTERVIEWED – BUT DIDN'T GET THE JOB!

If this happens, it can certainly be a disappointment ...especially if you were short-listed! Unfortunately, only one person can get any one job...*but* that successful candidate won't be around to compete with you next time - so you can go for the next job ahead of the field!

Nevertheless, you may be feeling puzzled, especially if you felt you were totally right for the job and that it was almost within your grasp. What could have tipped the scales in the other applicant's favour?

If you have been dealing with a reputable recruitment consultant, you can always ring and ask. Intermediaries are much more likely to give you honest feedback than the firm itself would if you were to speak to them directly. So feel free to ring the consultant involved and ask. It could be valuable knowledge that may help you in your future search.

Perhaps you were regarded as overqualified. Unfortunately, if you're too good for the job it can be just as bad as not being good enough! Chances are that, overqualified, you would end up feeling underpaid, unsatisfied and would soon have yourself on the market again. Such a situation is not good for the firm or for you. Short-term employees leave their footprints on CV's... and employers tend to be wary of them!

Personal prejudices and preferences, too, might have entered into the final selection process, especially if the contest was close.

If you were not perceived to be as relevant for the job as another applicant, realise that perception is really just another person's opinion. A different firm, a different job and different interviewers will yield different perceptions. Accept the situation and move on. Think of all the new jobs that have come on the market since you discovered the last one. Be assured that constant unrelenting perseverance will lead you to success.

Another thing worth remembering is that recruitment consultants are dealers in human resources...and they, like most dealers, have a passion for collecting the quality stuff! They won't let you slip through their fingers if they think there might be another more likely contender for your services in their network.

That dream job will not come from asking '*can* I make it?' but by stating - and truly believing 'I *will* make it!' If other people can do it, so can you. You now know what it takes, so...

GO FOR IT!

IF YOU ARE OFFERED THE JOB

Congratulations! Do you have your referees all teed up ready to extol your virtues when the recruiter rings them?

It's also a good idea to ask the new firm for **'A LETTER OF OFFER'** when they tell you the job is yours. Most firms will provide one; if yours does not, or the job level is not seen as warranting one, at least ask for a 'JOB OFFER' in writing before resigning your old position.

Now it's time to pack your briefcase and move on to the next chapter entitled: *How To Keep That Great Job!*

Good luck!

PART THREE

HOW TO KEEP
THAT GREAT JOB

ADJUSTING

Persistence has paid off! Now you can relax and concentrate on your new position...or can you?

The first few days in any new job can be traumatic. You are a stranger not only to the office operations but to your co-workers as well - and they are strangers to you.

There are going to be lots of toes to tread on protruding from under those desks, counters or machines. You, the unwary outsider, will inevitably step on some of them if you are not careful where and how you walk.

You will find that unseen boundaries exist marking other people's territory; it is advisable, therefore, not to risk encroaching until you know where those boundaries lie. People tend to guard their job territory and work relationships rather jealously. Until they get used to you and can reassure themselves that you are no threat, don't risk arousing their survival instincts.

Whether you plan to make a 'big splash' or swim quietly along in your new job, you'll need time to adjust to the culture and to your co-workers. Let them see you are consistently punctual, well-groomed, not pushy but pleasantly approachable. These are obvious ploys to settling in comfortably.

As time goes on, of course, you will no longer be an 'outsider' but one of the crew. You will find friends and allies and learn whom to trust.

Adjusting to a new work environment can be a little hard at first, especially in the area of management: you don't really know those you're supposed to be managing. It is like being made the conductor of an orchestra without having time to tune-up the instruments: you can't count on performance without discords. If you want harmony and no off-key surprises, allow time and patience for mutual adjustment. Whenever you feel you must issue a firm directive that doesn't go down too well with the team, try not to be authoritarian: do it in a warm and sympathetic manner that shows you really believe in what you are doing.

As a subordinate, getting to know your manager involves you showing right from the start that you are an eager and interested employee. It also requires tact and a little caution on your part. However, by courteously pursuing the directives given to you and making certain you understand your manager's intent by asking for clarification where necessary, you should have no trouble at all settling in comfortably.

Every new venture requires this 'settling in' period - so don't feel bad if your ability to adjust seems strained to the limit over the first few days. You'll soon get the hang of it all.

On the other hand, you may be so au fait with the position and its procedures due to extensive past experience that the new one seems like 'a piece of cake'. This gives you self-confidence and great ideas for changing things for the better. But...patience! There's nothing like breathing in the coal dust for a while until you gain a first-hand understanding of *why* things are as they are. Maybe, in the light of that understanding, your appraisal will be quite different. At least, you will have gained a better idea of the most effective method for altering these established paths without antagonising the conservatives.

If you cross swords with fellow workers, especially in the early stages, you can expect the sour grapes to last. It is said that first impressions count. When suggestions have to be made that are not going to please everyone, show you are genuine about what you believe, that you are not out to hurt anyone or tread on anyone's toes.

Remember filling in our initial questionnaire at the beginning of this manual? One of the first questions we asked was, 'what are your strengths?' Turn to this now and look over your answer. Can you put those strengths into operation in this new job? How?

To develop in the position, you need to recognise and build on those strengths so that you become 'expert' in some area or some field within your career. Read and learn all you can about making that expertise - whatever it is - even better, whether it's in the field of selling, marketing, management, interpersonal relationships etc...and become unbeatable in that area.

ON-THE-JOB NETWORKING

Intelligent networking can give you the power and ability to get things done more easily and efficiently and the strength of Superman. When you are faced with a problem or a challenge, you have dozens of sources from which you can draw assistance and support.

How do you network successfully? The essence of networking is 'reciprocity'. Go out of your way to be friendly and helpful with colleagues and competitors alike - and they will be friendly and helpful to you.

Networking is not only necessary within the firm; its value to you is greater the further it extends. People who succeed invariably 'have a friend who knows a friend who...' Even friendly competitors can be of value. So, depending on the type and level of job you have, don't underestimate the value of joining relevant networking organisations, clubs, seminars, wining and dining those you think may be of help to you in your work and following up on likely customers year after relentless year. This means, in total, taking every opportunity to earn the respect, esteem and helpfulness of every useful contact.

Never, NEVER miss meetings that you are expected to attend. Each time you go along is a chance to be seen and accepted as an integral part of the company scene and culture. More importantly, it is also your chance to put forward innovative ideas that you may have thought about and prepared well beforehand. Your constant input becomes invaluable.

If you hate speaking up in meetings or before a group or audience but it's part of your job, enroll yourself in a public speaking course or go along to your local Toastmasters' or Rostrum Club. They'll turn you into a pro before you know it. These meetings are generally well-structured and enjoyable. If you'd like to know more before joining, you can go along to one of their meetings, sit at the back and just listen.

Always try to attend a company's end-of-year party or ball if they have one - and any other business-related social events your organization puts on...no matter how tired you are or how boring they are. Remember, if you want to get ahead, the more you are seen supporting the organisation, supplying creative input and making yourself part of the corporate picture, the more indispensable you will become.

THE MANAGEMENT CULTURE

The management culture of an organisation simply means its modus operandi or 'ways of doing things'. It is important that members of an organisation understand the management culture if they are to be not only contributors but personally satisfied survivors.

How does this management culture originate? It springs from top management, reflecting its expectations on those who serve it. Not every detail of management culture can be decided at the top: descending levels of management take into account the wishes of top management yet have evolved their own 'ways of doing things'.

Managers are human but they vary markedly in management expertise. Some are leaders and others will never understand what leadership demands. However, most want to impinge their views or authority into the team and its operation. In reality, the sum total of the management cultures at various levels equates to the total management culture.

Which part of the employer organisation have you joined? Remember that each part has its own management culture believed to be in line with top management wishes. Both employer and external recruiter need to understand the nature of the overall and particular management cultures if the matching of a potential employee to the organisation is to be a continuing success.

Never be afraid to ask about the management culture, especially that at the point of entry to the organisation that interests you. It is a fact of life that you will not really know how that culture impacts on you until you have experienced it first hand: then you will have three options: a) accept and adapt to it; b) try to change it; c) reject it and resign!

Management cultures do change, believe it or not. The input by middle and lower management plus the changing views of top management about how to operate in changing economic and political circumstances all affect the 'way of doing things'. Sometimes there are big ructions at company Board level - just as in political or public service arenas - which reflect changing attitudes on the part of the powerful people in the organisation. These can filter down through the organisation's operational levels as changes (for the better or the worse) for your segment...and have an effect on *you*.

There is no need to be overwhelmed by management culture. For the beginner, it has less importance than for the more senior executive who must cope with in-house political problems. It always needs to be *understood* however as it is a significant factor in keeping a great job.

DISCRIMINATION IN
THE WORKPLACE

We like to think that discrimination or prejudice based on race, sex, age, religion or anything else is a thing of the past. Therefore it's quite a shock to the system if we do strike a problem of this nature at work, especially if it's from those on whom we depend for assistance, information or advancement.

Open blatant discrimination can be dealt with pretty smartly these days by going to the proper authorities and making a formal complaint. Covert discrimination is perhaps more difficult to cope with and is beyond the scope of this book.

However, a word of caution if you merely 'suspect' you are being discriminated against by an antiquated management, perhaps because you are never given any real opportunity for advancement or because you feel you are not shown the appreciation you deserve: you *could* be misreading your situation! Often such problems are not due to discrimination at all but to some other factor such as an employee's out-dated skills, slack work practices, poor communication or lack of some important personal quality necessary to the job like team spirit, assertiveness or good leadership...so it is pays to investigate first before coming to the conclusion that one is a victim of discrimination.

Discuss the problem with a couple of trustworthy colleagues to get their perspective. Then request your superiors to give you some feedback on your current assessment rating and, if they say it's not up to scratch, try to establish with them ways they feel you could improve it. Of course, if the prejudice you suspect is real, you may merely strike a wall of awkward silence or evasion when you broach the subject with them.

If there is no doubt in your mind that you *are* being discriminated against, what can you do?

Firstly, if you try closing your eyes to the situation hoping it will go away, you risk a long spell of unhappiness. If the discrimination is coming from upper management, you also risk stunting the growth of your career. Ask yourself: 'why *should* I have to put up with this misery and unfairness?' The answer is: *you don't*!

Should you change jobs? Having read this manual, you should have no trouble doing that whenever you want! - but, in resigning a job that you otherwise like and have every right to, you'll be running away from a situation that should not be permitted to go on...and should never have occurred in the first place.

In saying this, it is recognised that some gentle souls are simply unable or unwilling to cope with such unnecessary traumas - even if it is a matter of standing up for their basic human rights! All they want out of life is a peaceful existence and, for such people, moving out of such a negative and heartbreaking environment may be the only viable avenue to take. (It is preferable they not hand in their resignation until they have found a replacement job, however.)

What does this manual suggest if you are absolutely certain you are being discriminated against at work - either by management or individuals? It suggests you help to make the world a better place for yourself and others by taking AFFIRMATIVE ACTION! Broach the subject with management first in an open, genuine attempt to solve, rather than inflame, the potentially volatile situation - and then, if you get nowhere, go to the appropriate authorities (e.g. Human Rights & Equal Opportunities Commission), preferably with back-up from colleagues who have witnessed the problem.

Ask yourself, what have you got to LOSE by standing up for your rights? Only a job that is making you miserable! What have you got to GAIN by standing up for what you believe in? Self-respect, dignity and the knowledge that you are contributing to the sweeping out of the last vestiges of discrimination in the workplace!

EFFECTIVE COMMUNICATION

"In the right key one can say anything, in the wrong key, nothing. The only delicate part is the establishment of the key".

- GEORGE BERNARD SHAW

For centuries, humans have acknowledged that *the pen is mightier than the sword* - but they don't always have the skill or confidence to wield such an effective weapon. Good oral and written communication skills are worth acquiring if you want to keep - and enjoy - your job, no matter what level or field of employment you are in.

Communication among friends is easy and enjoyable. After all, one can choose one's friends. Communication among co-workers, superiors and subordinates is not a matter of choice but necessity. Yet there are ways...

On-the-job communication should be motivational, particularly in the management of subordinates - but also in 'managing' colleagues! You can't force people to see your point of view and you can ruffle quite a lot of feathers in trying to do so. It's pointless and time-wasting if the proceedings are stopped dead in their tracks while a battle of wills takes place.

If you don't agree with a colleague or subordinate on some point, ask yourself if there is *anything* he or she has said on which you could agree in order to find some common ground. If there is, highlight that agreement and use it as a stepping stone to get them around to your way of thinking.

Remember, too, the valuable art of compromise: e.g. "I agree with you that we need......x......but I also understand.....y! I wonder if a compromise solution would be to......z." Looking for compromises where possible - or at least agreeing to consider another's point of view - leads co-workers to respect you for listening to them and usually obliges them to at least consider what you have to say.

In meetings, it pays dividends to be as well-prepared and well-researched as you can be. If you need time to consider something or consult with others, say so. Even in emergency meetings where decisions may have to be made on the spot, you can still keep a pleasant face and think logically before presenting your views. Always, regardless of the conditions you're working under, try to be specific in making your point and hit the nail right on the head.

You will find these are all 'great' ways to keep a 'great' job...and become a 'great' employee!

However, remember this is an era of rapid change and enormous technological advances in every corner of the workplace. There is no way you can expect to keep a position if that job, or the firm, no longer exist.

You might make contingency plans to investigate the market for other jobs, update skills or learn new more appropriate ones... or even consider going into business for yourself...exist. This is where good networking comes in: not just to elicit favors or find yourself a better job if you want it but to be ever privy to what is going on about you in your work environment.

By keeping your 'ear to the ground', so to speak, you can be ever alert to talk of take-overs, make-overs, down-sizing and other possible nasties well before they occur.

You might make contingency plans to investigate the market for other jobs, update skills or learn new more appropriate ones...or even consider going into business for yourself...

PART FOUR

SELF-EMPLOYMENT
WOULD IT WORK
FOR YOU?

BE YOUR OWN BOSS!

You may have decided that you are no longer happy to work your life away for others while they rake in all the profits. People of any age or background can come to this conclusion. The alternative? A business of your own!

Don't be afraid of the thought. Increasing numbers of people are setting themselves up in their own businesses, some fulfilling lifetime ambitions, some looking for autonomy and freedom, others out of sheer necessity.

Unfortunately, many innocents have been lured into shonky deals and fast-folding franchises by clever salesmen and glowing advertisements. The road to 'becoming your own boss' can hold many traps for the unwary - which only means you need to keep your wits about you and thoroughly check out the 'facts' before you buy or start up any enterprise.

Rarely is the going easy in the initial stages of starting up a business, particularly in the first year or two. Nor will you necessarily escape a tyrannical boss because, where it's *your* money at stake, you may find yourself working under the hardest boss of all: *yourself*!

Yet, there are also huge benefits in having your own business, like having some measure of control over your life at last and, hopefully, a better quality of life...that is, if you are neither a procrastinator nor a workaholic!

The knowledge that you are building something with your own two hands that is yours and will yield future benefits for you and your family is a great feeling. For an organised, clear-thinking individual with an entrepreneurial creative streak, it can be a wise choice. And, as you will see in the section on *Jobs of the Future*, it could give you more security and job stability in the future than traditional employment.

Starting up a business of your own doesn't always have to cost the earth. Most licensed tradesmen, for example, are able to get into their own businesses for the cost of a few well placed advertisements (plus comprehensive insurance cover!) if they possess their own equipment and enough capital to cover materials. People who love to cook can run catering businesses from their own kitchens or make quiches and specialty gateaux for restaurants. Baby sitters, nannies, gardeners start up agencies from home. Ex teachers tutor privately. Accountants, real estate agents, dressmakers, potters, DTP and secretarial services work successfully from spare rooms or garages. Retrenched executives with specialised knowledge take on consulting roles.

Whether you have been just playing around with the thought of going out on your own, or you have firmly made up your mind to take the plunge, it would be worth your while responding to the following self-questionnaire. It will help to uncover your motives for wanting to go into business for yourself, give you some direction and hopefully act as a catalyst for your creative ideas.

SELF-EMPLOYMENT
QUESTIONNAIRE

- **Why do I want to be self-employed?**

  _____

- **I didn't like being employed by others because...?**

  (Come on, out with it!...)

  _____

- **I didn't like my last job because:**

  _____

- **The type of business I would like to go into is:**

  _____

- **Because:**

  _____

- **The businesses I have considered so far are:**

  _____

  _____

- **These are the fears I have about going into business for myself:**

- **Is there a good chance I could overcome these negatives?**

- **How?**

- **Do I have the necessary skills and experience I will need?**

- **These are the skills and experiences I know I lack:**

- **This is what I want to earn per year...**

    (Put down a preferred salary range and look at the above answer again.

    For the type of business you propose, is this a realistic and achievable figure?

    Is it excessive? Is it too conservative?)

- **Just how much money do I *need* to earn to cover my requirements?**

- **What do I want to do with the money I earn?**

  (Sure, you'll pay the mortgage, rates, electricity, cars, insurance, the children's education etc...and you'll need to plan for a comfortable future. But, beyond these necessities, try to fathom your main lifestyle goals and dreams.)

- **Do I want to travel in the future?**

- **If so, how? e.g. luxury cruise ship, economy air, train...?**

- **How *often* would I like to travel? Several times a year - or once or twice in a lifetime?**

- **What type of car am I aiming for? A Holden? A Porsche? A stable of vintage cars?**

- **How do I wish to entertain? On a grand scale... or am I the intimate 'Sunday-barbie' type?**

- **What financial commitments do I have to my children's education?**

  (Will you be sending them to an expensive private school, boarding school, public school, university? Or are they already grown up and off your hands?)

- **Are you childless?**

- **What other on-going or up-coming commitments need I consider eg dependent relatives etc?**

- **Should I consider going into a partnership or will I 'go it alone'?**

  (Partnerships, even between friends, are not noted for their long-term success. It takes a lot of managing, trust and understanding to make them work. Furthermore, partners need to be prepared to put in equal amounts of time and effort and take equal reward out of the business. Having said that, there *are* partnerships that work, and work well.)

HOW HIGH SHOULD
I SET MY GOAL?

By considering your financial commitments (both short term and long term) when considering your goals, you will come to a more realistic appreciation of the level of remuneration your new business needs to provide you with.

It is pointless making yourself ill slaving relentlessly year after year in an overly demanding and high-risk business if you are satisfied with the simple life, have no extravagant plans and no children to support.

On the other hand, if you want a marble-floored mansion and Ferraris for all the family, your business income and risk-taking will need to match those requirements.

The *type* of business you'd like to be in - food, consulting, clothing manufacturer, newsagency, cruise boat operator etc.- will no doubt offer many possible *levels* of entry and of operation. By considering your personal and family goals when making your business choices, you will be more likely to achieve a balanced life.

For example, let's assume you want a food business. What *level* of food business will suit you, your family and your finances? A part-time hot dog van at the beach? A coffee or sandwich shop? A high-class French restaurant? A fish 'n' chip shop?

There are scores of possibilities but, if you love the simple life, have no aspirations to live like the Great Gatsby and you like going to bed early and getting up early, then maybe a sandwich bar or small local cafe would suit you well.

On the other hand, if you're a prospective jetsetter with a massive retrenchment package or considerable savings who longs to live and retire in luxury, a thriving Deli or major restaurant may be what you aspire to, regardless of the huge effort - and risk - involved.

Remember, money is worth nothing until you use it. A vault full of dollars or a jar full of cents are of equal value if you can't do anything with them because worry and overwork have caused you to take a stroke - or killed you!.

Admittedly money has potential - and that is always a comforting thought, especially in old age. But if you've had to trade your health and happiness for it, what is its *real* value?

So many small business owners realise this too late. Don't let it happen to *you*.

Work out your lifestyle goals first - then
find a business to suit those goals!

FRANCHISES

Buying a franchise is like having it a bit both ways: you're on your own at last - but have the protective shield of a proven company to protect you somewhat from possible beginner's errors, ignorance and gullibility. You will still be functioning from under the thumb of a superior - for better or for worse - but it's *your* money you are playing with now.

And, no matter how creative and spectacular you may think your ideas, you will still have to work within the confines and limitations of the franchise.

In other words, buying a franchise will not give you immediate freedom *or* autonomy. Your business will be orchestrated by a 'father-figure' firm that already has a set business practice. It will be up to you to administer and manage your own outlet in accordance with the company's proven principles if you want to reap the same benefits as other successful franchisees.

Some franchises can fill your pockets with gold: others can line your boots with lead. Finding one that is going to be right for you and your circumstances will require patient research and observation.

Because of clever advertising and PR, some people are led to believe franchises are a license to print money. On the contrary, they usually entail very hard work for the franchisees...especially in the initial stages.

Your choice may be an established outlet or a brand new one. Either way, because it's a franchise, it will already have the value of name recognition, established performance, the expertise (hopefully!) of the franchisor, the benefits of group marketing and advertising...and that all-important hand of experience to help you over rough spots. Most respected franchisors have a vested interest in the success of their outlets.

But don't kid yourself. If you purchase a well-established outlet from a well-known franchisor, you may be paying huge dollars for it - and that is only the start! You've then got to staff and run it. You may find yourself working like a dog seven days a week for a very long time to make it viable. Are you willing to do this?

Remember, too, that if *they* go broke, *you'll* go broke! Before you do anything, talk in depth to other franchisees of the firm if at all possible to double check on what you've been led to believe - and to uncover any unknowns. Doing your homework now will pay dividends later. If you still decide to go ahead, you will be doing so with your eyes open - regardless of how prestigious the company name is.

Seeking advice (even getting second opinions) from relevant professionals - accountants, solicitors etc - before you sign on the dotted line could save you getting into something you can't handle financially, physically or emotionally.

BUYING A BUSINESS

The catch phrase here is 'buyer beware!' You should never, never buy a business on a 'walk-in walk-out' basis...or you might be the one walking out in a very short time with only the shirt on your back.

It goes without saying that your accountant is the one who should look over the books, regardless of the extra expense. Also, it is preferable that the vendor's solicitor is not your solicitor for this particular sale!

Find out, too, if the vendors are likely to be re-opening elsewhere. If they are, where will it be? Are they moving only a few streets away and taking with them the thousand loyal customers that you think you're buying from them? Just as the children of Hamlyn followed the Pied Piper, loyal customers tend to follow old established businesses if they are still within cooee. It's something that you need to consider and protect yourself against unless you are particularly well situated geographically - i.e. right in the hub of town.

To obviate possible competition from the vendor, get your solicitor to design a protective codicil for your contract requiring the seller to agree not to start a similar business within 'x' kilometres (or in the same suburb - or whatever you feel is fair) as the business you are buying. Don't be afraid to request this as the success or failure of your business may depend on it.

As in all buying and selling negotiations, the one with the money has the upper hand... and, at this point in the negotiations, that's YOU!

If you are so strapped for money that you can't afford a professional to advise you and help you produce a business plan, it may be safer to give up all thought of starting up on your own. Trying to put a new business on the road without a business plan or any real business knowledge is like trying to drive off in your car wearing a blindfold.

Make appointments to see your accountant, someone in the Small Business Centre and your bank to discuss the ins and outs of your proposal. There are many costs that can be overlooked - including how you are going to survive the initial start-up period if you're not the overnight success you hope you'll be.

PREMISES: LEASED OR FREEHOLD?

There is no all-time definitive answer here. Sometimes owning commercial property is a no-no: other times owning *any* property is a no-no. At the time of writing this, property is the only way to go! You need to do a fair bit of investigation before investing in the market.

Providing a lease is not too cumbersome - three years with three-year options is widely accepted - you have a chance to walk out at the end of three years if the going gets tough. However, if you *own* the premises and want to get out, you will either have to sell it or lease it to someone else. That could take a very long time. Some commercial properties lie vacant for years.

Generally, position is as big a consideration when it comes to leasing premises as it is in buying a freehold. Attractive rent or price is not always the heaven-sent opportunity it appears on the surface. If yours is to be a retail business that depends heavily on passers-by...and you never see a soul around that end of town...your business won't have a chance unless you have unlimited funds for advertising! You may pay more dollars to be strategically located in the middle of a shopping centre, but it could be worth it to you in the long run.

This does not necessarily apply to factories, *specialist* retail... or businesses that have real exclusivity. Such places can often function very well away from the expensive shopping strip once they become known - but it's advertising that will get you known in the first place.

If you propose leasing the premises, gather the following information and then see if your interest is still as strong:

1. How much are the outgoings per year? Is the owner or lessor expected to pay them?

2. Do the premises have good natural lighting or will the gloom necessitate your having the lights on all day?

3. Is there any evidence of leaks either in the ceiling or down the walls? If so, will the owners fix the problem before you move in and sign to that effect? Are there damp areas evident on walls or floor that may ruin your merchandise?

4. Is there sufficient customer parking nearby? Your premises might be highly visible - even on a main highway - yet all those passing cars will continue passing by if they cannot easily park or get off the highway. They'll notice you - you might even become a landmark with your fancy flashing signage - but nobody will stop and buy from you if they can't stop or park easily.Is there all-day parking for YOU? If you have to move your car every couple of hours throughout your working day, life will become impossible.

5. Is there all-day parking for YOU? If you have to move your car every couple of hours throughout your working day, life will become impossible.

6. Where are the conveniences? Way down the back in the wind and the rain? Will that worry you over a period of time? Will you have to lock the shop and tack a 'Back in 5 minutes' notice on the door every time you want to visit the toilet?

7. In Australia, summers can be hot - so check to see whether the roof is insulated. Unless the premises are overshadowed by other buildings, an iron roof could heat up and make life a misery in the summer...and increase your air conditioning bills.

THE GREAT LITTLE HOME-BASED BUSINESS

"A musician must make music, an artist must paint, a poet must write if he is to be at peace with himself," said psychologist Abraham Maslow.

"Nice work if you can get it - but who *pays* musicians, artists and poets to indulge in their dreams?" you may ask.

Lots of people... depending on the level of talent and how it is is *marketed*! The same goes for any other craft or trade. For example, a good portrait painter could choose to draw $5 portraits of passers-by in the mall... *or* set him/herself up in a thriving little well-advertised business in a home-studio selling portraits for $2000 or more a-piece! It's all a matter of being entrepreneurial enough to recognise a market 'niche' in your area of interest or expertise and taking advantage of it in the most cost-effective way. Thus you can incorporate job satisfaction into your necessity to earn *and* make a profit even from doing what you love.

More and more small businesses are being run successfully from home and thus are able to avoid large overheads. Most councils have no objection to this but there are certain limitations on the area of premises allowed for business, limits on noise and traffic, machinery permitted and size of advertising signage which must be observed. You may also have a problem if you need to employ outside help.

Usually, a spare room or garage is ideal for starting out in many service-type businesses, especially if it has its own entrance.

There are enormous lifestyle benefits in working at home such as no commuting, no parking problems, no commercial landlords to contend with and a timetable that is set by you. Maybe you can even wear a tracksuit and sneakers to work if most of your people contact is by phone.

However, there are a few things that new and inexperienced home-based entrepreneurs can overlook, possibly due to the sense of security that comes from working in such familiar territory.

For example, it's surprising how many people overlook INSURANCE COVER when they work from a home base. Theft, fire and accidents do happen! And clients don't check first to see if you have Public Liability in place before they trip over the hose! So do see you have all the necessary insurance as well as personal income protection, disability insurance, superannuation and so forth before you start.

There are a few other potential problems, too. For example, to be truly productive working from a home base, one needs to be extremely *self-motivated*. Procrastination is easy. Domestic and family affairs have a habit of assuming an urgency they would not otherwise have had if you were away at an office, factory or store. For some reason, the at-home worker has always been a sitting duck for friends, neighbours and family visits.

People often have the impression that, if you are your own boss and working from home, your work hours must be flexible. However, several small distractions - like coffee with a neighbour, a trip to the shop for milk or raking up those leaves all over the back lawn can add up over a day.

If you are going to succeed at home-based work, you will need to establish clear working hours with friends and relatives and a firm resolve that you will not be interrupted for any reason.

Yet - and many have found it hard to strike the balance! - in working at home solo day after day, you can miss the stimulus of having colleagues around with whom you can relate and discuss work issues. Social interaction with co-workers is acknowledged as being an important ingredient for creative planning and thinking. Alone and without such interaction, enthusiasm can wane and die.

Self-discipline, determination to succeed and real self-motivation are prime requisites for the self-employed. Few businesses are an overnight success: the history of most show a jigsaw of frustrating setbacks, deep satisfactions, hopes dashed and fulfilled, hard work and sheer joy. Staying power comes from taking the long-term view of success:

keep your eye on the target: not on the arrow!

OUTWORKING

Outworking offers an real plus for many people: it enables those with small children or aged and ill relatives to work at home. There is no marketing or selling as there would be if you were self-employed. You merely do what you are hired to do - piece-work, stuffing envelopes or whatever - and your mind is left free for other things.

However, to make anything like a living from it, outworkers need to work long hours and observe incredibly tight deadlines. This type of work tends to exploit the needy or deprived, paying workers a mere pittance for their labour. Most realise they are being exploited, of course, but are afraid to complain for fear of losing the only job that will enable them to stay at home. Others may also fear investigation by the Taxation Department or Social Security because their income is merely supportive to the family and so paltry anyway that they are reluctant to declare it.

Few good outworking opportunities exist; if you can find something that suits your current circumstances, take it only if you are housebound. It will seldom make you a millionaire! Besides, there are plenty of other better-paying opportunities if your circumstances allow you to get away from the house - cleaning and gardening for example Use your local paper: advertise yourself - or look for people needing such services.

It's amazing how many people are afraid to advertise their services, especially if finances are tight. The unfortunate fact is that generally you've got to spend money to make money. You can say quite a bit in a $25 local classified. On the other hand, if people don't know you're there or what you have to offer, how can they avail themselves of your services even if they need them?

One thing is certain, however. While you continue to do piece-work in the back shed for peanuts, you'll be nothing but a slave.

PART FIVE

JOBS OF THE FUTURE

INTERVIEW WITH TOP ECONOMIST PHIL RUTHVEN

In matters of the future, the name of economic forecaster Phil Ruthven (IBISWorld Chairman) has become a household word. His predictions for Australia's future, made primarily to enable strategic business planning for clients, have spilled over from boardrooms into the popular media and gained him a fascinated national audience.

When it comes to forecasting likely changes in the workplace over the next few decades, Ruthven does not see the same scenario that sci-fi writers seem to favour: a few super-intelligent human beings controlling a sea of robots and heavy hardware. Ruthven admits that predicting the specifics of the future job arena is not easy...even with the massive IBISWorld data base as his crystal ball...but he is confident he has the broad parameters correct.

He starts with the principle that virtually every industry is created through outsourcing. Industries and jobs in the economy are the result of somebody somewhere surrendering the doing of something they've been doing and allowing someone else to do it for them.

As he points out, this process began with the Agrarian Age where families outsourced growing their own food, which gave birth to the agricultural & fishing industry, subsequently supported by transport services, wholesaling and retailing (replacing bartering) and banking. He says that in Australia, this age started later than in many countries given the isolation of the aboriginal population and their Hunting & Gathering age until European settlement.

The Industrial Age, starting in the mid-1860s, discouraged us from making our own goods whereas, previously, we had been making everything for ourselves from clothing, furniture and farm equipment right down to our own bread and jam. Ruthven says: "In giving up making our own goods, we gave up half the unpaid work at home. That decision led to the mighty manufacturing industry that went on to employ a third of the workforce by 1960... and full employment!"

Australia's Ages Of Economic Progress

GDP @ Constant F2017 Prices   **1788-2018 and onwards**

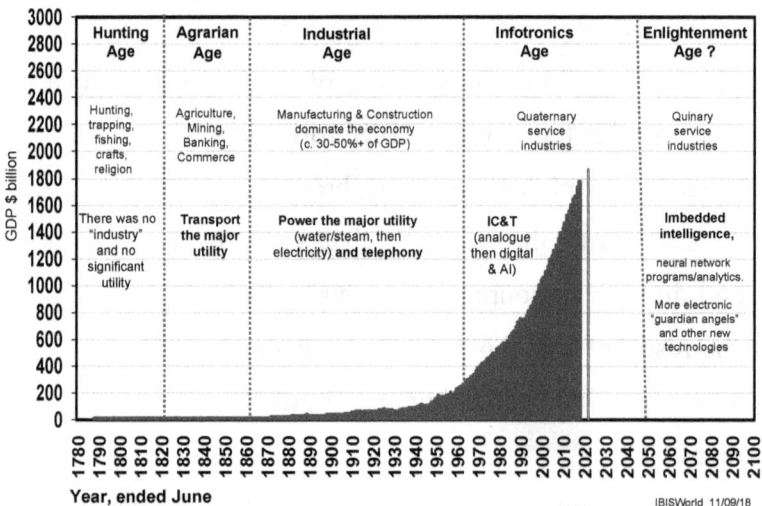

	Hunting Age	Agrarian Age	Industrial Age	Infotronics Age	Enlightenment Age ?
	Hunting, trapping, fishing, crafts, religion	Agriculture, Mining, Banking, Commerce	Manufacturing & Construction dominate the economy (c. 30-50%+ of GDP)	Quaternary service industries	Quinary service industries
	There was no "industry" and no significant utility	Transport the major utility	Power the major utility (water/steam, then electricity) and telephony	IC&T (analogue then digital & AI)	Imbedded intelligence, neural network programs/analytics. More electronic "guardian angels" and other new technologies

Year, ended June   IBISWorld 11/09/18

Now, in what many have termed the 'New Age', we're being encouraged to forfeit the other half of that unpaid work in the chores and services area.

Today, we let professionals perform tasks like mowing our lawns and cleaning our carpets. We're even giving up much of the cooking, too, and increasingly patronise fast-food outlets or have food home-delivered. Almost a quarter of our meals are now outsourced.

Ruthven says that in surrendering these tasks to others (some of which were kept as "therapies" or a hobbies), we have created millions of opportunities in outsourcing or sub-contracting these various services. "They have become full-time paid jobs for people willing to do them and are run on a far more organised basis than they ever were," says Ruthven who believes many service businesses are proving to be potential goldmines.

"For example, the concept of 'pick-up and return laundry and dry cleaning' has got to be an industry that will ultimately employ hundreds of people", he says, and has already begun in some high rise apartment blocks. "Alternatively we can outsource in-house cleaning, washing and ironing service providers".

In fact, Ruthven questions whether home laundries and kitchens will be worth having at all in twenty years time, except for basics like refrigerators and microwaves. He says the plethora of pick-up and delivery systems which will be available then could make them redundant.

The list below reminds us of the sort of outsourcing that has already taken place since the new age began in the mid-1960s, and which now employs over 3.5 million people (almost 4 times all employment in manufacturing) with a revenue in 2013 of some $310 billion, equating to average household spending on these services of $670 per week.   This was more than all spending in retail stores (except cars and related outlets).

Household Outsourcing in The New Age

Entertainment
- ❖ Hospitality Clubs
- ❖ Taverns, Pubs and bars
- ❖ Casinos, other gambling

Tourism
- ❖ Hotels, motels, guesthouses etc
- ❖ Entertainment centres, theme parks,
- ❖ Air travel, boat travel, car rental

Meals
- ❖ Fast Food outlets
- ❖ Theme Restaurants.
- ❖ Home delivery (of fast food).

Finance, Invest. & Legal
- ❖ Investment Advice & Mgt.
- ❖ Tax Planning & Returns
- ❖ Legal services

Health
- ❖ Wellness
- ❖ Home nursing, aged care at home.
- ❖ Home masseur treatment.

Childminding
- ❖ Nanny services, child minding

Maintenance
- ❖ Room/house painting
- ❖ Home Repairs
- ❖ Electrical
- ❖ Plumbing etc

Gardening/Exterior
- ❖ Landscaping, clean-ups.
- ❖ Lawn mowing
- ❖ Pool Maintenance.

Hair & Beauty
- ❖ Hairdressers/beauty salons
- ❖ Hair restoration

Sexual Services
- ❖ Sexual services

Cleaning
- ❖ Laundry, dry cleaning services.
- ❖ Internal cleaning.
- ❖ External cleaning

Car maintenance
- ❖ Detailing, oil changes, brakes etc

To take full advantage of the new service-oriented lifestyle awaiting us, service providers, too, will surrender their own mundane home chores to relevant professionals, he says.   A mowing franchisee, for example, may have his washing picked up by a laundry service while he is out mowing lawns and vice versa. According to Ruthven, both parties benefit.

What about the affordability of these services? "By working just one hour at something you're trained to do...and getting well paid for it...you can buy many other services that would take you hours to do yourself."

Businesses these days are also outsourcing what they term 'non-core' activities.

Business Outsourcing in the New Age

Trucking
- ❖ Road transport industry.

Cleaning
- ❖ Office, factory, hotel etc.
- ❖ Laundry, work clothes.

Canteens, Dining Rooms
- ❖ Caterers.

Maintenance
- ❖ Painting. Carpentry
- ❖ Engineering. .

Contract Mining

Agricultural Services

Security
- ❖ Security systems.
- ❖ Surveillance services

Personnel
- ❖ Recruitment.
- ❖ Out placement.
- ❖ Training.

Reception
- ❖ Serviced offices.

Accounting
- ❖ Payroll, Invoicing, Share Registers
- ❖ Full contract accounting.
- ❖ Superannuation administration.

Computing (ICT)
- ❖ Software development & writing.
- ❖ Computer services (IT outsourcing)
- ❖ Cloud computing

Property
- ❖ Property trusts,
- ❖ Property management

Marketing
- ❖ Advertising, media buying
- ❖ Call Centres

Distribution
- ❖ Warehousing & Delivery

Information & Planning
- ❖ Database services
- ❖ Strategic and Other Consulting

Other
- ❖ Franchising
- ❖ Other functions and activities

"Such outsourcing has created over 1.5 million jobs since the mid-1960s when the new Infotronics Age began."

And we should not forget that other countries can create jobs for us by outsourcing *their* needs to *us* as the list below reveals:

Overseas Outsourcing to Australia

Tourism
- ❖ Incoming visitors.
- ❖ Travel/booking services

IP & Business Services
- ❖ **Designs, patents** (eg. Orbital Engine Co).
- ❖ **Systems intellectual property eg. franchises, licences.**
- ❖ **Technical know-how.**

Education
- ❖ **Tertiary & lower education** (incoming students and outgoing teachers).
- ❖ **Electronic education** (satellite, diskettes, CDs, videos etc).

Health
- ❖ **Surgery and recuperation /sanatorium services.**

IC&T
- ❖ **Software, selected hardware, on-line information**
- ❖ **Meteorological information etc.**
- ❖ **Communication services**

Sport
- ❖ **Competitive** (regional & world events).

Manufacturing
- ❖ **Value-added resources.**
- ❖ **Downstream manufactures** (from resource strengths).
- ❖ **Unique manufactures.**
- ❖ **Services** (advisory).

Mining
- ❖ **Energy minerals** (oil, gas, uranium, coal).
- ❖ **Metals** (iron ore, alumina, nickel, gold).
- ❖ **Non-metallic** (rare earths).
- ❖ **Services.**

Agriculture
- ❖ **Crops** (cotton, new fruit & vegetable, sorghum, oilseeds, rice).
- ❖ **Livestock** (beef).
- ❖ **Fishing** (fish farming).

"Of course, in the case of international outsourcing, it is a two way flow. We *lose* jobs by outsourcing to overseas - particularly manufactures to China and other countries".

All of these new jobs, plus those created via the New Age utility of Information Technology & Telecommunications (ICT) and now Fast Broadband emerging as part of the Digital Era, have led to the following list of the nation's fastest growing industries.

Fastest Growing Industry Themes
New Age 1965-2040s

- ❖ **ICT & Fast Broadband -** the New Age all-pervasive utility.
- ❖ **Knowledge Industries -** databases & multi-media services.
- ❖ **Business Services -** outsourcing non-core functions.
- ❖ **Financial Services -** outsourcing of transactions/investment.
- ❖ **Property Services -** outsourcing ownership, facilities mgt.
- ❖ **Health -** outsourcing home doctoring.
- ❖ **Education -** outsourcing pre-school, plus universities.
- ❖ **Personal & Household Services -** outsourcing chores.
- ❖ **Hospitality & Tourism -** outsourcing the kitchen and travel
- ❖ **Recreation & Cultural Services -** outsourcing leisure.
- ❖ **Mining -** energy minerals (oil, gas, coal, uranium)
- ❖ **Construction -** cyclical, but growing importance of civil work
- ❖ **Transport –** cyclical, but growth in road, air, pipeline and F/F
- ❖ **Agribusiness in the North –** Asia's food security demand pull
- ❖ **Biotechnology & Nanotechnology -** New Age technologies
- ❖ **Environmental Services -** testing, assessment, amelioration

Moving to the question of business success in this new Century, Ruthven says it will depend not so much on having *capital* as having the right *ideas* and being able to recognise the needs of customers.

"Back in the early days of the Industrial Revolution, it was possible for people with very little capital to start up a business," says Ruthven. He excludes most of the 20th Century, when capital intensivity became the norm. "Today, it's the same story. You don't need a lot of capital - but you do need a fair degree of ingenuity.

"Now, however, instead of having to dream up clever gadgets like Edison with the light bulb, Bell with the telephone or Ford with the motor car, most of which were 'technological breakthroughs', in the New Age we'll be thinking up *new systems* and new ways of doing things quicker and cheaper but that depend *less* on equipment and technology and more on systems."

Work sharing, it seems, will play an increasing part in the new quality of life. "Part of this work-sharing is via a higher proportion of full-time jobs... three in ten today versus one in ten in 1946. In Holland, four in 10 jobs are part-time.

"Fifty years from now, we're looking at a full-time worker working three or four days a week at most - or six months of the year on and six months off. We'll only be doing two thirds of the amount of work then that the average person does today!

"But remember, we'll work for many more years than our forebears due to much greater life expectancy: we're just spreading the work out over more years. "Two hundred years ago, when we worked 65-70 hours a week just to survive, the average life expectancy was about thirty-eight years. We live twice as long now by the principle of *collectively* doing things - which one calls an 'industry' - rather than *individually* doing them - which is what we do in the home."

Although Ruthven believes working partly from a home base is already 'technologically and systems-wise' possible now. He feels the need will still be there to work gregariously with other people, both for productivity and for "bouncing around of ideas".

Interestingly, this gregariousness is also emerging via telepresence communications which is advancing to 3D and almost tactile levels. It is suggested that up to a quarter of the workforce will be working fully or partially from their homes by the middle of this Century.

This increasingly service-oriented lifestyle is expected to benefit just about everyone, affording more leisure time as well as longer life-expectancy.

"It's not only homes that will increasingly relinquish their mundane chores. Businesses, too, are already trusting a great deal to outside service providers. Many big banks and other big corporations no longer wish to carry large economics and other departments when they can outsource or subcontract their information needs to specialists.

Companies that have sprung up in the last hundred years are now so complex that they need to subcontract for simplicity of operation. There'd be at least another million or so jobs in subcontracting to big firms – such as courier services, cleaners, finding information, doing the firm's accounts and so forth."

Now for the bad news: Ruthven believes many professions could suffer with the move into a world of fuzzy logic, artificial intelligence and neural networks over the coming years. Law is just one example.

"Over three-quarters of the reasons we currently need lawyers is likely to be supplanted by automation. Conveyancing, for example, probably represents a good half of what lawyers were needed for thirty years ago. This can now be done over a computer at the real estate agent's office.

"You don't even need a lawyer for a divorce any more, although most will still do use them! In fact, if you look at all the things required of a lawyer fifty years ago, you'd have to say there are few of them left." Mind you, he says, that isn't stopping the growth of legal services in new areas such as litigation (personal and corporate), mergers and acquisitions, international legal matters etc. And the legal services industry remains huge, with revenues over $20 billion and employing tens of thousands.

A much tougher situation exists with manufacturing. 'Today we drive a car that has electronics all through it - so much more sophisticated than a car of twenty years ago. Yet we employ only about a quarter of the number of people we once used to make *more* cars *more* sophisticated to do *more* things! Soon, Australia will not manufacture cars at all due to a lack of economies of scale, importing all of them. We're close to that now yet the economy, jobs and our standard of living keep rising.

"In the past, we tended to believe a professional job required more cerebral power or I.Q. than an industrial or craftsman-type job. That's not going to be true in the future. In fact, I think we're going to be in for a big shock. For example, in our own work at IBISWorld, we're finding we can turn high quality work of a highly sophisticated nature in information through using high school graduates as well as economic and graduates from other diciplines!

"This is showing up time and time again in New Age learning situations such as software writing, information science and commerce.

"Universities really became giant technical colleges after the war", says Ruthven, "a place for a 'meal ticket' entry into a well-paid job! Now, they're finding the amount of information which world-best-practice companies themselves have is far outstripping much of the knowledge in a university - and it's more up to date.

"People training to go into fast food businesses, for example, get a more practical education at McDonald's than by going to a TAFE College. As it turns out, one can get formal qualifications (TAFE) from such companies these days. Similarly, if you want to learn business economics, theoretically a year at IBISWorld would do you more good than *three years* at university...it's more up-to-date with more modern equipment and techniques.

"For companies to survive today, they have to be super-modern, super-well-equipped and super-intelligent. And the better ones are miles in front of any TAFE college or university."

As for teachers, Ruthven sees three traditional roles: 1) imparters of knowledge, 2) tutors and 3) custodians. "It's possible teachers will even lose their tutoring role, too, because the tutoring capacity of the modern computer will be better than the vast majority of teachers. In forty or fifty years' time, teachers will be merely facilitators and custodians... except for adult (>18) students, of course."

How important are computers expected to become in our oives this new millennium? "Most people will use a computer in almost any job they tackle in the 21st century but a computer, after all, is just a black box. Already the cost of a computer is virtually down to less than the cost of a cheap T.V. set. It's the software that's doing all the work. Software is not technology. Systems, the way jobs are organized: that will be what matters!

"For example, Microsoft, the world's biggest software company, is growing faster than IBM. IBM makes the box but Microsoft invents the system that goes into the box. Big corporations these days often pay more for the software that drives their computers than they do for the hardware. And the advent of "cloud" computing services takes this trend to yet another level of sophistication, convenience and lower costs.

"People regard the invention of electricity as having been vital to the Industrial Revolution - and indeed it was. But the thing that turned out to be more expensive was the machinery that *used* the electricity.

"Today, it's not the hardware that's expensive but the software, telecommunications (we are using so much of it in data form) and the systems that 'hang off' it that cost much more than the raw technology. I think this is one of the hardest concepts for anyone to come to grips with, whether it's the man in the street or at corporate level."

Ruthven is emphatic that the New Age is not about machines, gadgets, boxes and so forth. "It's about intellectual property, neural networks, fuzzy logic, cognitive computing and analytics.

"However", he stresses, "ICT (information, technology and telecommunications) is a 'utility' in the same way as the telephone, electricity, gas and water were utilities back in the Industrial Age.

Their most important role is facilitating other industries, new and old, rather than creating new jobs in their own right."

Ruthven says we are already into the 'New Age': he sees as the 'fourth leap' in the evolution of humankind. The first was the age of hunting and gathering. The second, the Agrarian Age, bringing with it the capacity to live in cities for the first time. The third was the Industrial Age that removed the really hard physical work from people's lives.

The New Age will extend to the middle of this century, he says. He terms it the 'Infotronics Age', the age in which information, electronics and intellectual property reign supreme over physical property. And after that?

"Then we'll enter what I'd call the Age of Enlightenment which will be the 5th great step forward." At this point, Ruthven says our focus will have well and truly changed from the pursuit of material goods to an emphasis on living longer - over a hundred years! - and have healthier lives and the getting of wisdom and intellectual pursuits.

He refers to the well-known triangle drawn by American psychologist Abraham Maslow (1908 - 70) to illustrate man's *Hierarchy of Needs.* At the base, Maslow placed things absolutely essential to life like food and shelter; at the top, ne placed what he called the 'higher order of needs'. "Once you eliminate the basic fears of not being fed, clothed or healthy, you are free to philosophise and speculate on life's mysteries...such as the Meaning of Life and so on."

Ruthven points out that this pattern has already started to emerge in the form of our willingness to fight for *causes* such as the environment, women's suffrage, the right to vote, Gay Rights and so forth. "We saw a massive expression of all that post 1960, thanks to the reforming zeal of the Baby Boomers"

One might ask 'so what's new?' The Greeks were into causes and intellectual curiosities thousands of years ago.

Ruthven says the difference is that now it involves a much higher proportion of people. After 1965, even though we had two-income families, we didn't use that extra income initially for leisure or thinking time...only to acquire more physical assets: larger homes, two cars, other goods...and more services!

"We probably frittered away much of the discretionary time we otherwise would have had in the pursuit of burying ourselves with things we thought then were important...but now we're beginning to wonder whether they were!

"People are starting to look for a simple life. They're going for apartments rather than the 25-40 square homes. They ask: 'why *should* I bury myself in possessions?' Values are shifting noticeably."

Ruthven predicts the swing to a much more philosophical, discussion-oriented future will not be easy to handle at first.

"However, fifty years from now, you'll find those generations that have grown up with computers, software, systems and intellectual property will have 'been there, done all that!' We'll be writing more and more clever software, and trying to move in and value the *wisdom* end of the spectrum. "In fact, just thirty years from now, the philosophy and logic of the past 4000 years will seem like kindergarten stuff!" he says.

If Ruthven is right in his predictions, the technology of the future is nothing to be feared. On the contrary, it promises to be the very tool that will free us to fulfill our role of what it is to be truly human.

PART SIX

DO-IT-YOURSELF
RESUME GUIDE

SETTING OUT THE RESUME

PLEASE REVISE THE FOLLOWING CHAPTER BEFORE BEGINNING THIS PROJECT:

Preparing Your Resume (Pg.39)

It is important for you to know that there are many ways one can set out a resume.

If you have never before written a resume and are not sure of how to word it, you will be doing yourself a great service if you can afford to have your first one professionally prepared.

However, for the purpose of Do-It-Yourselfers, this guide offers an easy and relatively foolproof format which you might wish to use as a template for your own career details.

You will notice that some personal details are optional…

PERSONAL AND CONFIDENTIAL

RESUME OF (Your Name)

PERSONAL DETAILS:

Full Name:
Address: (Optional. Rarely given at this stage)
Telephone: (Mobile)
Email:
Date of Birth: (optional - but it's usual to put it in!)
Marital Status: (optional)
Leisure Interests: (Don't list too many. The idea is to
                                show you're a focused, well-balanced
                                individual, neither predominantly
                                introverted nor extroverted.)

CAREER PROFILE: (Just one paragraph giving a summary
                                of your skills and experiences to
                                date - or how you see those skills and
                                experiences in relation to your next
                                career move. Its purpose is to let the
                                recruiter see at a glance that you're at
                                least relevant for the job.)

EDUCATION:

TERTIARY
University or Institute:
Final Year: (year)
Qualifications   (Degree/Diploma/Certificate/Incomplete)
Distinctions: (If any)
Posts of Responsibility: (If any)

SECONDARY
School Attended:
VCE/HSC (or final year)
VCE/HSC Subjects: (ONLY if you have recently left school
                           or have a very short work history! You
                           could list your HSC subjects & results
                           as below:)
                           (Subject 1) Result:
                           (Subject 2) Result:
                           (Subject 3) Result:
                           (Subject 4) Result:
                           (Subject 5) Result:
Distinctions: (If any)
Posts of responsibility: (If any. If you've just left school, you
                           might mention responsibilities you
                           had at school such as School Captain,
                           Editor.)

FURTHER
QUALIFICATIONS   (List any other courses you've
                          completed: mention languages acquired
                          and other skills. IT skills are often
                          so important to certain jobs that they
                          deserve separate mention. If you're
                          short on skills or qualifications,you
                          could include any part-time or
                          voluntary work you've done.)

PROFESSIONAL ASSOC
/MEMBERSHIPS:

EMPLOYMENT HISTORY

(Start with your most recent position and work backwards in reverse chronological order. Note: information should be supplied for each job you nominate, with most information about your current job if you are still employed or your most recent job if you are no longer employed.)

COMPANY NAME:
Date started - date left:
Description: (Few sentences describing the company services/products, number of employees, office locations)

Position(s) held:
Responsibilities: (Include reporting to, number of employees directly managed - if relevant)

Achievements: (If relevant)
Reason for Leaving:

(After you've listed all necessary information about the companies you've worked for, finish with the following:)

REFEREES

Supplied on request   (You will ultimately need to supply
                              2-3 referees but, for the moment, you
                              can merely state: 'Referees supplied
                              on request'. However, before you go
                              along to interview, you will need to
                              obtain your referees' permission before
                              revealing their names and contact
                              details. They should all be people who
                              can - and will – speak knowledgeably
                              about your professional and personal
                              qualities.)

Index